T0328870

ITALIAN PROSE USAGE

ITALIAN PROSE USAGE

A Supplement to Italian Grammars

BY

WALTER SHEWRING
(M.A., Oxon.)
Assistant Master at Ampleforth College

CAMBRIDGE
AT THE UNIVERSITY PRESS
1948

CAMBRIDGE
UNIVERSITY PRESS

University Printing House, Cambridge CB2 8BS, United Kingdom

Cambridge University Press is part of the University of Cambridge.

It furthers the University's mission by disseminating knowledge in the pursuit of education, learning and research at the highest international levels of excellence.

www.cambridge.org
Information on this title: www.cambridge.org/9781316509685

© Cambridge University Press 1948

First published 1948
First paperback edition 2015

A catalogue record for this publication is available from the British Library

ISBN 978-1-316-50968-5 Paperback

CONTENTS

CONTENTS

PREFACE

THIS BOOK is addressed in the first place to those who are learning to write Italian and who feel the need for some assistance in passing from the merely correct translation of sentences to continuous composition of an advanced and serious kind. I assume these students to have already mastered some good small grammar (Grandgent's, I think, is the best I know), and to be accustomed to using the large edition of Hoare's 'Italian Dictionary'; and I try to provide such further information as experience has shown me to be most called for. Since most of those who learn Italian have previously learned French, I have thought it well to note some resemblances and differences between the two languages. And I have relied a good deal on the use of quotations—often extended ones—from modern Italian authors; these serve to exemplify not only the constructions considered but also the tone and the contexts in which such constructions are used.

I may well be reproached with incompleteness. The elasticity of Italian makes it specially hard to codify; doubtless there are accidental omissions, and in any case I have consciously passed over certain exceptions to my rules. But I hope that the work will bridge a gap and encourage the student to investigate further upon his own account and by means of his own reading. In such reading he will be well advised to pay special regard to Tuscan usage. For general technique, the structure of paragraphs, sentence-rhythm, there are many non-Tuscan writers—Albertini, for instance, and Ojetti and Pirandello—who are excellent models for the writing of modern Italian prose; but for some refinements of detail the standard lies with Tuscans alone, and in such matters a Collodi or Fucini is more to be respected than a more sophisticated author of wider reputation. And if one should honour Tuscan usage, much more should one shun journalistic usage—I mean such locutions as *rimarcare* for *osservare* and *arrangiare* for *mettere a posto*. An Englishman's Italian will in any case have weaknesses or stiffnesses enough; but at least he may choose his reading carefully, and he should be under no temptation to adopt such vulgarities as these.

Furthermore, I hope that the book may be of some service to those who do not write Italian but have occasion to read it or translate it. The common level of knowledge here is notably low. Scholars in other fields fall into strange pitfalls when they have to use Italian works; and respectable journals which have acquired some awareness of *faux amis* in French are content to write 'loyal' for *leale* or to take *contrasti* as the simple equivalent of 'contrasts'. Such ignorance (and, by implication, such indifference) does not help to cement international goodwill.

Had I had the leisure and facilities, I should have liked to complete the book with some annotated passages for translation and corresponding fair copies. The scheme has been thwarted for the present, and I can only hope to return to it when time and circumstance are more favourable.

I am deeply indebted to the Mistress of Girton, Miss K. T. Butler, for her general encouragement of my work and her detailed help in revising and amplifying the manuscript.

W. S.

I

VERBS

General importance of the verb

§ 1. The verb in general is more important in Italian than in English. Modern English, like modern French, throws more and more weight on nouns, on abstract nouns especially; Italian inherits from Latin a preference for more concrete expression through verbs. We shall return to this more than once [see especially §§ 20–1, 61–2, 92(f) (ii)]. Here meanwhile are a few examples:

> They arranged a **meeting**.
> *Stabilirono d' incontrarsi.*

> What is the **price** of **admission**?
> *Quanto si spende per entrare?*

> Any **complaints**?
> *C' è da ridire?*

> His book is a **reflection** of..., an **epitome** of....
> *Nel suo libro si rispecchia..., si riassume....*

> In the **diffusion** of this knowledge Baretti's **influence** was important.
> *Baretti molto potè a diffondere la conoscenza....* (Praz.)

The contrast made here is of course not absolute. In any given example one could probably use English verbs and Italian nouns. Nor has Italian quite escaped the modern international jargon of scientists, politicians and journalists in which ambiguous abstract nouns jostle each other from start to finish. But the BENT of Italian favours verbs; a normal passage of good Italian will contain more verbs than the corresponding English; and the student should learn to work through them rather than through nouns.

Alternative forms of the verb

§ **2.** (a) Sometimes, but not too often, one should make use of the 'apocopated' verb forms: *amar, vien, amavan,* etc. Such forms must never be used before a pause (unless one is writing verse); they require another word to lean on ('*Così fan tutte!*' but '*Tutte lo fanno!*'). And they are not much used before vowels; many of the best Italian writers favour the 'hiatus' (more strictly, synaloepha) of, for example, *andare ancora* as against *andar ancora.* The following points are a rough summary of modern usage, and concern those forms only which almost any writer might use. It will be understood that particular writers have their own preferences in these matters, and also that the shortened forms are in any case rarer than the full forms. I call *amar* a 'very common' form relatively to a form like *devon,* not to *amare*; e.g. the same writer might use *amare* three or four times for one *amar,* but *devono* twenty or thirty times for one *devon.*

(i) The shortened infinitive is very common. In particular, *far* is generally used before another infinitive (*far venire* rather than *fare venire*); but the full form should be kept before *s* impure.

(ii) In the present tense, *son* for *sono* (1st singular or 3rd plural) is very common indeed. *Par, vien, vuol* are all common, but other such 3rd singular forms are rare. The shortened 3rd plurals most used are those of common verbs whose shortening gives monosyllabic forms: *van, dan, fan, stan, san*; *devon, lascian,* etc. are much rarer. Shortened 1st plurals are used less and less, though *siam* and *abbiam* may still be found in some writers.

(iii) In the imperfect, *avevan* and *eran* are not uncommon; *andavan, credevan,* etc. may be used cautiously.

(iv) In the past definite, such forms as *andaron* are now rare.

N.B. Students should beware of imitating Manzoni's very free use of apocopation; it was exceptional in his own time, and goes far beyond the practice of modern Italian.

(b) 1st person imperfect in -*a*. Throughout his 'Grammar', Grandgent inexplicably prints *aveva, parlava*, etc. as the normal 1st person form; he then adds (p. 56) that *avevo, parlavo*, etc. are 'nearly always used in conversation, and occur often in the works of modern authors'. As the student will have discovered, this is an understatement. The form in -*o* is of course the normal modern form. In written as in spoken Italian, the form in -*a* is highly exceptional, and when used has probably to be eked out by *io*. It is best avoided altogether.

(c) Contracted -*ea*, -*ia* for -*eva*, -*iva*. This form, once very frequent, is now almost obsolete except in *avea*, which is sometimes used by writers who would never think of using, for example, *dovea* or *sentia*. The plural -*ean* is rarer than the singular; but Fogazzaro has *Ne avevan parlato*, **avean** *disputato molto*.[1]

(d) To these points I may conveniently if loosely attach a note on the alternative position of pronouns after finite tenses of the verb (e.g. *trovasi* for *si trova*).

(i) In the present tense, *Vendesi* and *Affittasi* are current in notices and advertisements. In literary Italian, this position may still be used with a few short and common verbs in the 3rd singular reflexive: *Trovasi, dicesi, leggesi*.

(ii) In the imperfect, an occasional use of this position is or has been favoured in careful prose, especially in descriptive passages (more perhaps in the last generation than in this). Within these limits, it is common with *si* and 3rd person singular, considerably less common with *si* and 3rd plural; it is also still used at times with other pronouns and with adverbs (e.g. *trovavalo, andavanci*), but too rarely for imitation.

The following examples are typical, and may well be imitated in translating English of the same general tone:

> *Mentre l' alba si accendeva in aurora, la fronte di Franco* **venivasi** *irradiando di una luce interiore, gli occhi suoi ardevano, fra le lagrime, di vigor vitale*. (Fogazzaro.)

[1] Cicognani uses these contracted forms with unusual freedom.

*L' ombra **addensavasi**, il vento urlava sempre più forte, con un continuo rombo di tuono.* (Deledda.)

*Lo spazio...era singolarmente lungo, vuoto, e quasi un deserto lucido e pauroso. La stoffa della vasta portiera **agitavasi** ancora dal basso in alto in tutte le sue pieghe, tanto violentemente ella l' avea traversata.* (Bontempelli.)

Tenses of the indicative

PRESENT

§ 3. Present for past definite. This 'historic present' is commoner in Italian than in English, though probably rarer than in French. Its use needs no illustration.

§ 4. Present for future.

(a) In main clauses. When English allows a present in a future sense, Italian allows it too. 'I leave (I'm leaving) to-morrow', *Parto domani.* Notice the common phrase *E adesso come si fa?*, 'What do we do (shall we do) now?'

Italian is even a little freer in this respect than English. Thus one may say *Domani vengo a trovarti*, 'I'll look you up to-morrow'; *Vo a vedere*, 'I'll go and see'.

(b) In subordinate clauses. English uses present for future in conditional and temporal clauses. Italian allows the present in conditionals, disallows it in temporals. Thus:

> If he comes, I shall see him.
> *Se viene* (or *verrà*), *lo vedrò.*
>
> When   } he comes, I shall see him.
> As soon as}
>
> *Quando*} *verrà* (or *sarà venuto*, but not *viene*[1]), *lo vedrò.*
> *Appena*}

---

[1] To be frank, the present does occur even in temporal clauses. Verga has: *Appena arriva la balia, non avrete più bisogno di me.* And Bontempelli: *Appena arrivano, li farete entrare qui* (though just after: *quando saranno arrivati, potete andare a dormire*). But this use of the present is exceptional; it might be called lax, and is certainly better left alone.

FUTURE

§ 5. (a) The future may indicate probability. This idiom exists in English, but is much commoner in Italian. When an Englishman hears a clock strike, he may say 'That'll be ten', but he is as likely to say 'That must be ten' or 'That's ten, I expect'. The Italian formula is in each case: *Saranno le dieci.*

(b) A slightly different and un-English use: the future may indicate possibility or concession.

> *Sbaglierò, ma...*, 'I may be wrong, but....'
> *Sarà vero, ma non lo dovresti spiattellare così.* 'It may be true, but you shouldn't blurt it out like that.'

N.B. *Stare* (*essere*) *per* is a common periphrasis for the IMMEDIATE future. Its exact equivalent is 'to be about to'. Modern English prefers 'to be going to', but this formula is more flexible than the Italian. 'He is going to sing' may mean that the song will follow at once or that it is to be sung at a concert next month; *Sta per cantare* means the former only.

IMPERFECT

§ 6. Since Englishmen are often in doubt when to use the imperfect in any foreign language, it seems worth while to discuss the matter at some length.

English has three common forms of the imperfect tense:

> I was talking.
> I used to talk.[1]
> I talked.[2]

In translating the first two forms there is no difficulty whatever. If English has 'I was talking' or 'I used to talk', then the Italian equivalent is naturally *parlavo*.[3] The question is: If English says 'I talked', are we to use imperfect or past definite, *parlavo* or *parlai* ?

---

[1] With 'I would talk' as a rare variant.

[2] With of course the negative form 'I did not talk'.

[3] It may sometimes be desirable to bring out the continuity of 'I was talking' by translating *Stavo parlando*; or the habitual quality of 'I used to talk' by translating *Solevo parlare* or *Parlavo di solito.*

The general answer is this: If the action of the verb is thought of as repeated (habitual) or continuous, the imperfect is to be used; if the mere action is considered, the past definite is to be used.

An important distinction: the point is not whether the action WAS IN FACT continuous or repeated, but whether it is SO THOUGHT OF by the speaker or writer. Most actions take an appreciable time, and if all that mattered were the mere fact of continuity or repetition, verbs like 'continue' or 'persist' would never be used in the past definite at all. We may now consider some examples.

§ 7. In main clauses:

> A. He slept that night for ten hours.
> *Quella notte dormì per dieci ore.*

> B. He generally slept for ten hours.
> *Dormiva di solito per dieci ore.*

> A. Yesterday I lost my way several times.
> *Ieri perdei la strada a più riprese.*

> B. He often lost his way several times in one day.
> *Spesso perdeva la strada a più riprese in un giorno.*

In both sets of sentences we are actually told that the action was continuous or repeated; but in the A sentences we are only concerned with the action ('What did he do? What happened?'), whereas in the B sentences we cannot think of the action apart from its habitual or characteristic qualities ('What were his habits? What kind of man was he?').

In these examples, certain words give a clue to the tense—'that night' and 'yesterday' in the A sentences, 'generally' and 'often' in the B sentences. But if we take an example with no such clue—

> He read 'Hamlet' with great enjoyment

—we can see that in a proper context the sentence would show itself as distinctly A or distinctly B. If all that matters is what the man did (he read 'Hamlet' for the first time, spent a particular evening in doing this), then we have an A sentence and 'read' is *lesse.* If we are thinking of the action as habitual or repeated or characteristic

6

(he read 'Hamlet' every so often; that is how he felt about Shakespeare), then we have a B sentence, and 'read' is *leggeva*.

In DESCRIPTIVE (as distinct from NARRATIVE) passages, the past tense is usually imperfect because the action of the verb cannot be thought of except as being continuous. Take for instance this: 'Dense fog **hung** over the city. People on foot **walked** gingerly, taxis **crawled**, policemen **seemed** to have lost their confidence.' All these verbs are B, for the writer recounts not just what happened but what was the state of things, what things looked like—and this cannot be thought of except as something continuous. Turn from description to narrative, and the verbs become A: 'Dense fog **covered** the south yesterday. Trains **arrived** hours late. The Channel service **was cancelled**.' Here the writer is concerned only with what **happened**.

In many sentences, the form 'I did' in English might be replaced by the form 'I used to do' or 'I was doing'. When this is so, the sentence is certainly B; but some B sentences do not allow of the substitution, for English idiom is somewhat elusive here. Thus in our first group of B sentences we could certainly write 'he used to sleep' and 'he used to lose his way' instead of 'he slept' and 'he lost his way'. In our second group we could write 'A dense fog was hanging'; we should be less likely to write 'people were walking' or 'taxis were crawling'; and 'policemen were seeming' is quite impossible. Yet all these verbs are equally B. The test is the question: Are we concerned only with the fact, with what happened, or must we consider also some characteristic or circumstances (what someone's habits were, what something looked like)—things that form the background against which more definite happenings occurred?[1]

The translation of 'was' has particular difficulties; it is often hard to decide between *fu* and *era* because either makes good sense. Thus Boccaccio in his Life of Dante says (A): *Fu il nostro poeta di*

---

[1] An alternative test suggested to me is this. Is there any indication (explicit or implicit) when the action began or ended? If there is, use the past definite. If there is not, use the imperfect.

When repeated actions take place over a LIMITED period of time, even if it is a long one, the past definite is frequently used, e.g. *Durante tutto l' anno* 1930 *feci ogni domenica una passeggiata in campagna.*

mediocre statura. Now we might well write (B): *Era di mediocre statura*, but with a slight difference of sense. The form *fu* indicates 'Here is a fact about Dante'; the form *era* indicates 'This is how Dante looked to his contemporaries', and a modern Italian writer would be more likely to take this point of view.[1]

§ 8. In subordinate clauses. The principles are the same. A few examples should be sufficient:

> When he came in, the others were asleep.
> *Quando entrò, gli altri dormivano.*
>
> When the cat was away the mice would play.
> *Quando non c' era il gatto, ballavano i topi.*
>
> The house was robbed while he slept.
> *Mentre egli dormiva la casa venne spogliata.*
>
> All the time he talked he made feverish gestures.
> *Man mano che discorreva, gesticolava febbrilmente.*

§ 9. We have dealt so far with the NORMAL use of the imperfect—the only important use. There are two other uses of which something must be said, since the student will certainly meet with them in his reading, though he is not bound to use them himself. We may call them the conditional imperfect and the historical imperfect.

§ 10. The conditional imperfect. The imperfect indicative may be used in one or both halves of a conditional sentence, replacing the pluperfect subjunctive or the past conditional. Thus if we wish to translate the sentence 'If he hadn't come just then, I should have drowned', we have a choice of four forms:

(a) *Se non ci fosse capitato in taglio, io sarei affogato.*

(b) *Se non ci capitava, io affogavo.*

(c) *Se non ci capitava, io sarei affogato.*

(d) *Se non ci fosse capitato, io affogavo.*[2]

---

[1] Leaving *fu*, as a friend remarks, for the kind of facts that might figure on a tombstone.

[2] Further examples of (b), (c), (d): (b) *Se non facevo così, ci arrivavo io solo quassù e la facevano a me la pelle* ('they would have killed me'). (Borgese.) (c) *Se non mi tenevo alla maniglia della porta, sarei andata in terra quanto son lunga* ('I should have fallen full length'). (Tozzi.) (d) *Se il facchino non l' avesse sostenuta, cadeva.* (Fogazzaro.)

(English has an incomplete parallel in such phrases as 'I was a dead man', common in certain conversations of fiction.)

The same use occurs fairly often in independent conditional sentences with *dovere*, *bisognare*, etc.; *dovevano*, *bisognava* may replace *avrebbero dovuto*, *sarebbe bisognato*.

§ 11. The historical imperfect. This is a kind of vivid substitute for the past definite, and is used where the past definite might in fact be used. It occurs most often in historical narrative, and generally in a group of similar sentences, e.g.: *Nello stesso anno* 1789 *succedevano eventi di scopo assai diverso; l' orientalista Jones* **metteva** *in luce la prima traduzione di un classico indiano; Mozart* **creava** *il più squisito dei quintetti;* **scoppiava** *la rivoluzione francese.* The imperfects here are not descriptive; they mean, not that these things were in process of happening, but that they happened; in fact, they correspond to the A sentences, not to the B sentences, of § 7.

It is difficult to distinguish the force of this imperfect from that of the past definite itself. We may say perhaps that it expresses something of this kind: 'If we look at the happenings of this year, we find Sir William translating, Mozart composing, the Revolution breaking out.'[1]

This explanation seems to the writer unsatisfactory; if to the reader it seems no explanation at all, he is advised to leave the idiom altogether, to cling firmly to the distinctions made in § 7, and in such a sentence as this to write: *successero, mise, creò, scoppiò.* The past definites will be correct.

PAST DEFINITE AND PAST INDEFINITE

§ 12. The main difference between *feci* and *ho fatto* is that between English 'I did' (past definite of the A form in § 7) and 'I have done'. This is not the whole truth. Italian sometimes uses a past indefinite where English would not, in reference to the *recent* past, e.g. *Ho fatto una gita ieri*, 'I went for a ramble yesterday'; this is fairly common

---

[1] French has the same idiom; in historical writing especially, *naissait, mourait* may have practically the sense of *naquit, mourut*.

in speech. And on the other hand, *lessi* in written Italian has some-times the force of 'I have read'.[1] Nevertheless, English usage is a safe enough guide, and it would be correct to say *feci* in the one case and to write *ho letto* in the other. French usage is different, and the student should not be influenced by it. For although, as has been said, the Italian past indefinite in conversation is sometimes an alternative to the past definite, it is not a necessary substitute as in French.[2] Italians have no feeling against the use of the past definite in speaking, just as they have none against the use of the imperfect subjunctive.

N.B. The past definite of certain verbs has sometimes a stronger meaning than other tenses: *Ebbi*, I got;[3] *fui*, I went;[4] *conobbi*, I met (made the acquaintance of); *seppi di...*, I was told of....

PAST ANTERIOR

§ 13. The past anterior is used much as in French.

(a) In subordinate clauses. After *appena* (*che*), *subito che*, *tosto che*, *quando*, *dopo che*, *poi che*, when the main verb is PAST DEFINITE.

> As soon as I'd got in, I saw what had happened.

$$\left.\begin{array}{l} \textit{Appena} \\ \textit{Tosto che} \\ \textit{Subito che} \\ \textit{Quando} \end{array}\right\} \textit{fui entrato},^5 \textit{ m' accorsi dell' accaduto.}$$

---

[1] Two modern examples. *Come un vecchio forzato che espiò* ('has expiated') *largamente la sua colpa ed è in pace con sè.* (Cecchi.) *Le parole hanno un potere proprio e una tentazione; e chi non ebbe ad arrossire d' averne abusato* ('has never had an occasion to blush')? (Bacchelli.) But this use is much rarer now than it was in the last century; cf. the past definites in Foscolo's preface to his '*Gazzettino del Bel Mondo*' (*intitolai...posi...disposi*—all past indefinite in sense).

[2] More exactly: In conversation and letters the past indefinite is preferred when one names a time which has not yet elapsed: *Ho fatto una gita oggi, stamane, questa settimana*. But if the time named has elapsed (by at least one clear day), Tuscans prefer the past definite even in conversations and letters: *Feci una gita ieri, la settimana passata, il mese passato.*

[3] *Scese all' Albergo del Sole, ebbe una stanza dove non c'era nè sole nè fuoco.* (Fogazzaro.)

[4] *Con un grido d' amore angoscioso Iride fu a lui* ('rushed up to him'). (Bacchelli.) *Fuggì, e fu nella stanza del figliuolo* ('entered his son's room'). (Panzini.) [5] Often abbreviated to *Entrato che fui*.

In such sentences the pluperfect should never be used.[1] But in familiar style one may use a past definite in the temporal clause, e.g. *Quando entrai*;[2] or one may substitute a participle for a clause, e.g. *(Appena) entrato, m' accorsi....*

When the main verb is IMPERFECT or PLUPERFECT, the subordinate verb is the ordinary pluperfect.[3]

> When he had got into bed, his mother would come and read him stories.

> *Quando*
> *Tosto che* } *si **era** coricato,*[4] *veniva la mamma a leggergli fiabe.*
> *Dopo che*

> When he had come in, he had seen what had happened.
> *Appena **era** entrato, s' era accorto dell' accaduto.*

(b) In main clauses. Here the past anterior is used chiefly after an adverb or adverbial phrase meaning 'soon'. Something of its force may be suggested by translation.

> *In un momento **ebbe** aperto il pacco.*
> In a moment he had the parcel open (RATHER THAN 'had opened the parcel').

> *In breve si **furono** scambiate le notizie.*
> The exchange of news was soon over (RATHER THAN 'News had been rapidly exchanged').

---

[1] Though the student should not be surprised to find some examples of it in his reading. A pluperfect may emphasize continuity, e.g. *Un giorno, dopo che s' era parlato* ('we had been talking') *più a lungo del solito, salì in camera mia.* (Papini.)

[2] E.g. *Appena riebbe l' uso della parola, cominiciò a dire....* (Collodi—though he has just above: *Appena maestro Ciliegia ebbe visto quel pezzo dì legno, si rallegrò tutto.*)

[3] It is sometimes forgotten that this is also the rule in French. Cf. Flaubert ('*Un cœur simple*'): *Dès qu'elles avaient dépassé les balises, elles commençaient à louvoyer.... Quand elle avait fait à la porte une génuflexion, elle s'avançait sous la haute nef.*

[4] Sometimes abbreviated to *coricato che era.*

PRESENT AND PAST CONDITIONAL[1]

§ 14. In indirect speech, the past conditional usually replaces the present conditional after a main verb in the past.

> She left word that she would be back in half an hour.
> *Lasciò detto che **sarebbe tornata** fra mezz' ora.*

Tornerebbe is possible but less usual.

§ 15. In main sentences, the present or past conditional is used to show that the statement is second-hand or not vouched for by the writer.

> By all accounts, he $\begin{Bmatrix} \text{is} \\ \text{was} \end{Bmatrix}$ the guilty man.
>
> *A quanto si dice,* \
> *Secondo voci che corrono,* $\Big\}$ *questi* $\begin{Bmatrix} \textbf{sarebbe} \\ \textbf{sarebbe stato} \end{Bmatrix}$ *il colpevole.*

> If Lamb is to be believed, only an impediment in his speech prevented him from becoming an actor himself.
> *Se gli si deve credere, solo un vizio della favella gli **avrebbe impedito** di diventare attore lui stesso.* (Praz.)

§ 16. The present conditional is often used as a polite understatement for the simple present. *Come sarebbe a dire?* 'You mean...?' And whereas Englishmen in shops generally say 'I want...', Italians say *Desidererei....*[2]

Tenses of continuity with *da*

§ 17. Here we consider the translation of such sentences as 'I've been living in London for ten years' and 'I hadn't seen him for a month'. Grammars state the rule correctly, but not explicitly enough. The rule is that when in such a sentence the action is given as still continuing, Italian uses the present with *da* for the English perfect and

---

[1] Throughout this book I have found it convenient to treat conditionals not as a separate mood but as tenses of the indicative.

[2] There is a ripe example of this kind of conditional (exceptionally transferred to the past) near the end of the first chapter of '*Piccolo mondo antico*'. The piano-tuner says: *Veramente, signora marchesa, io avrei già pranzato,* which means approximately: 'If I may presume to mention it, I've dined (lunched) already.' And in another passage ('*Leila*', ch. 12), Fogazzaro himself comments on the idiom: '*Xe (=È) pronto?*' '*Sarìa (=Sarei) pronto, sissignor*' *rispose il sior Momi con un condizionale pieno di esitazione riguardosa.*

the imperfect with *da* for the English pluperfect. This is true; but many students forget to ask themselves whether in a particular case the action continues or not; they would be ready at first sight to translate the sentences above as *Abito a Londra da dieci anni* and *non lo vedevo da un mese*. This would be premature.

Review the sentences in these differing contexts:

(a) 'I've been living in London for ten years, and I'm not going to leave it now.'

(b) 'I can't tell you what a relief it is to be in the country again. I've been living in London for ten years.'

(a) 'I hadn't seen him for a month, so I was surprised to hear he'd just died.'

(b) 'I hadn't seen him for a month, so yesterday when I met him I was shocked at the change in him.'

In the (a) sentences the action (or non-action) is continuous. The Londoner is still in London, the man who had not been seen has not been seen even now. Here the suggested translations would be correct.[1]

In the (b) sentences the action (or non-action) has been broken. The Londoner has escaped to Sussex, the man who had not been seen has been seen at last. Here the suggested translations would be wrong. In such cases as these, Italian has the same tenses as English (with either *da* or *per*). For the (b) sentences one should therefore write:

Ho vissuto a Londra da (or *per*) *dieci anni.*
Non l' avevo veduto da (or *per*) *un mese.*

There is the same distinction of tenses in subordinate clauses where the meaning is given without *da*, e.g.:

(a) *Dopo tre settimane ch' io non la vedeva, andai a trovarla.* (Foscolo.)

(When he went, he had still not seen her.)

(b) *Quando l' incontravamo per la strada, dopo qualche giorno che non s' era visto, gli domandavamo....* (De Amicis.)

(They saw him before they spoke.)

---

[1] Though, as a matter of fact, even in sentences of this kind some Italians use the 'English' tenses.

The infinitive

§ 18. The infinitive is used far more in Italian than in English. In particular it may replace (a) an English noun, (b) an English gerund, (c) an English clause.

§ 19. (a) The infinitive replaces an English noun.

We are not concerned with those infinitive forms which are also literal nouns in the sense that they may become plural, e.g. *il dovere*, 'duty', *il potere*, 'power', *il parere*, 'the opinion' (these have the plural forms *i doveri, i poteri, i pareri*). Quite apart from these, any Italian infinitive may become a noun through the addition of an article or demonstrative, and Italian idiom often prefers such infinitive-nouns to abstract nouns in the strict sense.

§ 20. Infinitive-nouns as subjects or objects of the verb. This is a common use, e.g. *Il suo gesticolare era goffissimo* ('his gestures'), *Aspettarono il levar del sole* ('sunrise'), *Quel continuo andare mi fece male* ('the continual motion'). The only restriction is that modern Italian does not favour an infinitive with article if a plain infinitive will serve instead. Thus the forms *era difficile crederlo, preferisco stare in piedi* now usually replace ...*il crederlo,* ...*lo stare in piedi.*

§ 21. Infinitive-nouns as objects of prepositions: equally common. *Sull' imbrunire*, 'at dusk', *col succedersi de' fatti*, 'with the sequence of events', *dall' imperversare della rivoluzione*, 'by the fury of the revolution'. There is often a series of such infinitive-nouns, e.g. *Adesso col frantumarsi dei così detti generi, col decadere o meglio con lo svenevole ripetersi della pittura sacra..., col credere che l' arte sia un mero piacere..., male si distinguono e s' intendono lo scopo e la ragione dell' arte* (Ojetti). 'With the disintegration..., the decadence..., the sickly repetition..., the belief....'

A few set phrases use the infinitive as a noun without the article: *a lungo andare*, 'in the long run',[1] *a suo credere*, 'in his opinion'.

---

[1] But *al peggio andare*, 'if the worst comes to the worst'.

14

§ 22. (b) The infinitive replaces an English gerund. This use is straightforward and well known.

> Digging is hard work.
> *Il vangare è una gran fatica.*
>
> I get more tired with writing than digging.
> *A scrivere ci duro più fatica che a vangare.*
>
> He ended by saying....
> *Finì con dire....*[1]

§ 23. (c) The infinitive replaces an English clause:

(i) In indirect statement. The infinitive with *di* is used instead of a clause to refer to the subject of the verb. *Disse di volere...*, 'he said that he wished...'; *Credo di potere...*, 'I think I can...';[2] *Se avessimo saputo di sbagliare,* 'If we had known we were wrong'. This is the ordinary usage.

Less commonly nowadays, the infinitive without *di* is used in indirect statement instead of a clause with *che*. The rules for the order and case of personal pronouns are important; they apply not to this construction only but to others, mentioned below in (ii), which also allow of infinitive-subjects distinct from sentence-subjects. The rules are: The infinitive precedes pronouns which are its own subjects; pronouns of the first and second persons are always in the nominative; those of the third may be in either the nominative or the objective.[3]

> *Sapevo non esserci rimedio.*
> I knew there was no help for it.
>
> *Dissero aver torto io e lei ragione.*
> They said I was wrong and she was right.

---

[1] Or *col dire*; but *per dire* is a Gallicism.

[2] Distinguish this from the elliptical use *Se credete di pranzare,* 'If you feel like dining'. In the latter idiom (which a translator may sometimes miss), *credere* means 'to think it best, right, proper, a good idea'. So *Come crede,* 'As you please, as you think best'.

[3] According to Fornaciari, they should be in the objective case if distinct from the sentence-subject, in the nominative if they coincide with it; but this rule is simply not borne out in the practice of good writers. On the other hand, it may be remarked that *lui* is likely to be preferred to *egli* if emphasis is desired. *Non si vergognava di ricorrere alla frode, pur d' esser lui il vincitore.* (Papini.)

This construction is unsuited to the familiar style (which uses instead a clause with *che*); in formal writing it should be used discreetly; some authors favour it, others rather avoid it. Here are some modern examples:

> *Capiva non esservi risposta.* (Bacchelli.)
>
> *Era chiaro essere lei all' estremo delle sue forze.* (Alvaro.)
>
> *Nessuna persona ragionevole saprà dimostrarmi aver io peccato d' infedeltà.* (Fogazzaro.)
>
> *Credeva il casellante avere a che fare con un folle.* (Pea.)
>
> *Asseriva non poter l' uomo esser mai certo di aver trovato il vero.* (Papini.)
>
> *Cencio s' era preso* ('had begun to wrangle') *col Nardini, il quale sosteneva essere impossibile anche per un professore il decidere....* (Fucini.)
>
> *Tu avresti detto questi non esser certo un uomo ordinario.* (Praz.)
>
> *...la trincea nemica, invisibile ma che mi dissero correre lungo la mulattiera....* (Soffici.)
>
> *...volendo che confessassero non esserci in tutto il mondo donna più bella dell' imperatrice della Mancia.* (Papini.)
>
> *È naturale che in Provenza si sia certi essere stata Laura a condurre il Petrarca all' immortalità; e che noi al contrario si creda essere stato il Petrarca a immortalare Laura.*[1] (Ojetti.)
>
> *Lo Schiller disse la musica esprimere l' anima; lo Schelling, contener essa le forme delle idee eterne; Giorgio Hegel, essere il suo dominio superiore a quella della vita reale; il Lamennais, significare la musica i tipi eterni delle cose; il Vischer, esser essa lo stesso ideale.* (Graf.)
>
> *Guerre sante e crociate, diceva perplesso don Giuseppe, farsi, quando mai, contro turchi e saracini ed altri infedeli...; Dio non aver confidato il suo volere a barnabiti missionari*

---

[1] On the other constructions involved in this example, see §§ 46–7 and § 26.

> *di libertà; sapersi intanto per certo che il Santo Padre,*
> *benchè amico dell' Italia..., non voleva la guerra con*
> *nessuno.*[1] (Bacchelli.)

(ii) In adverbial uses of various kinds. Sometimes English usage
allows a similar construction with gerund or infinitive,
sometimes only a clause.

A parlar così ti farai detestare.

If you talk like that (OR by talking like that) you will get
yourself disliked.

> *Giulia...credette che, a non rispondere subito, l' avvocato*
> *avrebbe voluto forse non prendere più la causa. Poi,*
> *a passare da bugiarda in quel momento, non ci sarebbe*
> *stato più rimedio.* (Tozzi.)

She thought that if she did not answer at once, the lawyer
might refuse to go on with the case. And if she seemed to
be lying then, nothing could be done about it afterwards.

> *L' ambiente paesano della Calabria, che gli è famigliare per*
> *avervi egli trascorso la sua infanzia.* (Antonini.)

...a background familiar to him through his having passed....

> *Il nemico non era più ormai così terribile da non poter noi*
> *tentare un poco il gioco di azzardo.* (Soffici.)

The enemy was not so formidable now that we could not...
(OR too formidable for us to...).

> *...qualche lezione privata con cui aumentava il gruzzolo per*
> *poter vivere, egli in Napoli, sua madre e sua sorella in*
> *provincia.* (Serao.)

...a few private lessons with which he eked out his hard-won
savings so that he could live in Naples and his mother
and sister in the provinces.

> *Neanche a domandarglielo, non diceva mai....* (De Amicis.)

Not even if one asked him would he ever say....

---

[1] From '*Il mulino del Po*', vol. I. These are the reflections of a parish priest
when two Barnabite fathers are preaching a 'holy war' against Austria.

So che Alessandro fu un po' offeso di non averlo io avvertito della mia partenza. (Nievo.)

I know that A. was rather put out that I gave him no notice of my departure (OR at my having given him...).

Meglio trovare una scusa plausibile di quel non andare nessuno de' due a trovarla. (Pirandello.)

Better to find a plausible reason why neither of them went to see her (OR for their joint failure to visit her).

Anna ne approfittava [*di questi momenti*]...*per fare qualche ricamo dei più semplici; per non spendere troppo e per non saperli fare meglio.* (Tozzi.)

Anna turned such time to account by doing embroidery of a very simple kind (this to reduce expense and because she lacked skill for the better work).[1]

OTHER USES OF THE INFINITIVE

§ 24. As an impersonal imperative. Commonest in public notices and book-references: *voltare a sinistra; vedere pag.* 251 (so also in French). The negative of this—for example, the *non sporgersi* of railway carriages—must not be confused with the twin formula (*non far così, non ti sporgere*) which is the negative imperative of the 2nd person singular. When people in crowds shout *non spingere*, they are not calling anyone *tu*—the meaning is nearer to 'no pushing' than to 'don't push'.

§ 25. Historic infinitive with *a*[2] (like the French historic infinitive with *de*, but of commoner use). This indicates the speed or abruptness with which an action sets in, and is often introduced by *e* (meaning 'and then', 'and at this', 'hereupon').

    Così disse; e tutti a rabbrividire.

    E il povero Geppetto a corrergli dietro. (Collodi.)

    E il cane a saltargli addosso e a scagnare come una creatura che capisce. (Fucini.)

---

[1] Notice in this example the elastic use of *per. Per fare=facendo; per non spendere=perchè non spendesse; per non sapere=perchè non sapeva.*

[2] Very rarely, *a* is omitted.

§ 26. *Essere a* with infinitive may replace a relative clause.

> *Fu egli a dirmelo.*
> It was he who told me (= *Chi me lo disse fu lui*).

> *Io credo che siano stati loro, quelli della giustizia, a rubarmi il sacchetto.* (Deledda.)
> I think it was the police who stole the bag.

> *Non c' è dubbio; è stato il postino a spargere la voce che io sono un 'signore'.* (Panzini.)
> It was the postman who spread the report....

§ 27. The infinitive is used in deliberative questions: *Che fare?* 'What was I (he, etc.) to do?' Also with *se*, indirectly: *Dubitava se restare o fuggire.* Also with interrogative and relative pronouns and adverbs, much as in English.

> *Non sapeva a chi fidarsi.*
> He did not know whom to trust.

> *Un amico a cui fidarsi.*
> A friend on whom to rely (a friend to rely on, a friend to trust).

> *Aveva compiti a cui attendere.*
> He had tasks to attend to.

> *Non seppe quel che rispondere.*
> He did not know what to answer.

[Note that after *sapere* Tuscan usage prefers *quel(lo) che* to *che cosa*.]

> *Il cuore mi doveva dire che cosa fare e che non fare.* (Borgese.)
> *Girava attorno lo sguardo cercando un luogo ove nascondersi, un appiglio a cui abbrancarsi.* (Albertini.)

§ 28. The infinitive with *a* may sometimes replace an English participle, e.g.:

> *Stavo a sedere (a guardare, a cucire).*
> I was sitting (looking, sewing).

> *Non staranno molto a tornare.*
> They won't be long getting back.

> *Rimasero a chiacchierare.*
> They stayed on gossiping (NOT 'to gossip').

§ 29. Anticipatory infinitive. An infinitive at the beginning of a sentence sometimes anticipates the main finite verb (usually an imperfect). The effect is of emphasis, often of contrast.

> *Leggere, egli leggeva molto, ma poi non ci capiva un' acca.*
>
> He read a good deal, as far as that went, but he simply made nothing of it.
>
> *Guardare, sì, lo guardava; ma lo vedeva poi davvero?* (Pirandello.)
>
> He was looking at it—no doubt about that; but did he really see it?
>
> *Stancare no, non si stancava mai la Generalessa; ma certo quanto più si va in là, eh?, più si va piano.* (Pirandello.)
>
> Of course she never got **tired**, but....

Such an infinitive may be preceded by *per*.

> '*Oh, e il mio elmo? dov' è?*'
>
> *L' elmo è il cappello. Lo ha, sì.* **Per averlo**, *lo ha; positivo.* (Pirandello.)
>
> (He can't have **lost** it, but where has he put it?)

Participles and gerund

§ 30. The present participle.

(a) When the present participle is used in a real verbal sense, it has the force of a relative clause. It is not equivalent to a gerund. Thus in the sentences *Era questo un libro* **contenente** *molti racconti stravaganti, Videro dei quadri* **rappresentanti** *scene diverse*, the participles could not be replaced by *contenendo, rappresentando*; but they might well be replaced by *che conteneva, che rappresentavano*.

The verbal use of the present participle belongs to the literary style, and even there is not common;[1] in conversation, and in ordinary writing, a relative clause is used instead. (It may be added that a great number of Italian verbs are deficient in present participle.)

---

[1] It is commoner in Fogazzaro than in most modern authors. Here are three examples from '*Leila*': *la folla dei grandi castagni* **scendenti** *per la costa; una nobile figura di donna...***spirante** *dignità signorile; casucce...***porgenti** *fresche ombre di viti sui vicoli.*

(b) The participle with article may become a noun; this is common enough in such phrases as *i viventi, i morenti, gli assistenti, il rimanente* ('the remainder'), *l' occorrente* ('the requisites').

(c) Commonest of all is the participle as a pure adjective: *ridente, piangente, commovente, consolante.*

§ 31. The gerund (present tense).

The gerund replaces the present participle in various adverbial uses—modal, temporal, conditional. It is never the mere equivalent of a relative clause [see § 30(a)].

(a) The gerund referring to the subject of the sentence.

> *Campava suonando il violino.*
> He earned his living by fiddling.
>
> *Passeggiando, mi incontrai con un amico.*
> I met a friend when I was out.
>
> *Lo farò potendo.*
> I'll do it if I can.

(b) The gerund used absolutely with no subject expressed.

The gerund may be impersonal, e.g. *Lo farò occorrendo* (= *se occorrerà*), 'I'll do it if necessary'. Or it may be personal, referring to an implied subject which is not the subject of the sentence, e.g.:

> *Frugando la casa, si ritrovò il cimelio nel palco morto.*
> When they searched the house, the precious object was found in the lumber-room.

(Notice that this construction passes as good Italian, though 'Searching the house, the treasure was found' cannot pass as good English. But 'searching' is felt as a participle only, whereas *frugando* has something of the force of a Latin ablative gerund.[1] In early Italian one could say *in frugando*.)

Further examples:

> *Atene fu presa risparmiando vite ed edificii.* (Panzini.)
> Athens was captured with much saving of life and property.

---

[1] All the same, the stricter Italian grammarians would scarcely approve of the construction, and the examples given should perhaps not be imitated.

Finì la cena, scambiando rade parole. (Bacchelli.)
Supper ended with little exchange of words.

Cenando, fu ventilato il progetto di visitare Pomposa. (Panzini.)
Over supper, the plan was discussed.

(c) The gerund used absolutely with subject expressed.

This corresponds to the present tense of the English nominative absolute, but Italian uses the construction more than we do. N.B. The gerund precedes its subject; pronouns of the 1st and 2nd persons are in the nominative; those of the 3rd person in either nominative or objective.

Crescendo il parapiglia, i bambini strillavano sempre più forte.
As the confusion grew, the children screamed louder and louder.

Stando io un po' discosto, non potevan vedere quel che scrivevo.
Since I kept to one side, they could not see what I was writing.

§ 32. The past participle.

Italian has three kinds of past participle which are usable separately: passive, intransitive, and reflexive. Once a verb is compounded with *essere*, its past participle may be used in its own right. Thus, since one says *È stato ferito, Fu scacciato*, one may also say *ferito*, '(having been) wounded', *scacciato*, '(having been) expelled' (passive). Since one says *Sono andati, La roba è costata lire otto*, one may say *andati*, 'having gone', *roba costata lire otto*, 'stuff which cost eight lire' (intransitive). Since one says *Mi sono svegliato, Si è accorto dell' errore*, one may say *svegliatomi*, 'having woken', *accortosi dell' errore*, 'having noticed his mistake'.

There also exist of course the longer forms *essendo stato ferito, essendo andati, essendosi accorto*, but there is no need to use them unless for clarity or for emphasis.

(a) Participle in agreement with subject. Different kinds of participle may be combined, and this is a great resource in narrative, e.g.:

Nato a Parigi e vissutovi parecchi anni, fattosi soldato e ferito nell' ultima campagna di Napoleone, recatosi poi in Inghilterra, morì a Londra nel 1830.

He was born in Paris and lived there for some years; enlisted, and was wounded in Napoleon's last campaign; then came to London and died in 1830.

Further examples:

> *Nato esule, trasportato fanciullo da luogo a luogo..., vissuto lungi dalle parti e dalle magistrature....* (Carducci.)

> *Scappato di casa a dodici anni, imbarcato a tredici, carcerato a quattordici, stato un pochetto pirata in mari lontani....* (Bacchelli.)

Such participles may be preceded by a conjunction, e.g. *Era triste* **perchè** *abbandonato;* **benchè** *scoraggiati, rimasero fedeli; sarebbe stato punito* **se** *preso.*

(b) Absolute past participle. This corresponds to the past tense of the English nominative absolute, but is often used where English would have either a participle agreeing with the sentence-subject or else an adverbial clause. Also, English often has a present participle where Italian prefers the more logical past participle. N.B. The participle precedes its subject, and pronouns of all persons are in the objective case.

> *Detto questo, se n' andò.*
> Having said this (OR, MORE LOOSELY, saying this), he left.

> *Morto te, dove andremo a finire noi?*
> When you are dead, what will become of us?

Further examples:

> *Finito il pranzo, accesi i sigari e le sigarette, si ragionava....* (Ojetti.)

> *Costeggiate le mura di Belisario, passata porta Pinciana, abbandonato il margine terroso del galoppatoio, Mario ed Elena senz' altre parole raggiunsero piazza di Siena.* (Bontempelli.)

> *Gli altri, scambiate abbondanti cerimonie con il dottor Záupa e fra loro..., lodato sommessamente, timidamente, il meraviglioso aspetto giovanile dei canapè, delle seggiole*

e delle poltrone, evocate con rispetto le ombre congiuntevi degli Záupa preistorici, cantata in coro la gran bontà delle stoffe antiche, non sapevano più che dire. (Fogazzaro.)

Tagliati gli spaghi rossi dei suggelli; aperta la busta...; estratto il quaderno di spessa carta...; sfogliate le due prime pagine..., monsignor Manassei in piedi, asciugatesi le labbra con una pezzuola di batista, cominciò la lettura. (Ojetti.)

The absolute past participle is sometimes preceded by *dopo* or *a*. Thus instead of *finita la cena* we may say *dopo finita la cena* or *a cena finita*. Note that when *a* is used, the noun precedes the participle and the article is dropped.

In a few phrases, the absolute past participle has no subject expressed: e.g. *Sparecchiato* (or *Dopo sparecchiato*), *si misero a giocare*. 'When the things were cleared away, they began a game.'[1]

§ 33. Passive participles of semi-auxiliary verbs.

The semi-auxiliaries *volere, dovere, potere, sapere* (to which may be added *finire* and *(in)cominciare*) are sometimes used in the passive voice when the passive sense belongs not to them but to the succeeding infinitive, e.g.:

Fu dovuto seppellire lontano da' suoi.
He had to be buried....

La folla non fu potuta trattenere.
The crowd could not be checked.

The corresponding participles may therefore be used in the same way: *Un disgraziato, dovuto seppellire...; una folla non potuta*

---

[1] Some grammarians would explain most of these examples as abbreviated forms of the 'past gerund' referring to the subject of the sentence; e.g. they would say that *Detto questo, se n' andò* stands for *Avendo detto questo, se n' andò*. This is arguable; but the only decisive examples of such a use are those where the participle is followed by a conjunctive pronoun, e.g. *Presomi per mano mi portò in una camera piena di sole* (Cicognani)—a construction which is sometimes useful. A sentence of Fogazzaro neatly unites this with other participial uses: *Presa la sciarpa, andò fiutando le orme di Teresina e trovatala, spiegatole il perchè del suo ritorno, la pregò di fargli vedere la chiesina, non ancora visitata.*

trattenere. It will be seen that such participles have the force of relative clauses ('who had to be buried', 'which could not be checked'); and it sometimes happens that they make a neat substitute for relative-forms too clumsy to use. Thus, *Stracciò la lettera incominciata a scrivere, Mi confidarono delle opinioni non volute esprimere a quegli altri* are a neat way of saying 'the letter he had begun to write', 'opinions they had not been willing to express'; but no one would think of using in the full relative form such a passive as *che era stata (da lui) incominciata a scrivere.* An ACTIVE relative form might of course be used instead.

The subjunctive

§ 34. There can be no question here of explaining or summarizing all uses of the Italian subjunctive. The following notes deal chiefly with usages which have been neglected or misunderstood.

§ 35. Independent Subjunctive.

(a) The 3rd person present subjunctive for imperative (*Me lo dicano Loro, Così sia!*) and the imperfect and pluperfect subjunctive of wish (*Fosse pur vero! Ci fossimo stati noi!*) are sufficiently well known.

(b) The imperfect subjunctive is also used as an INDIRECT imperative.

> *La gente rideva.... Ridessero.* (Bacchelli.)
> People laughed at him. Well, let them laugh.

> *Piero lo interruppe.... Facesse il comodo suo.* (Fogazzaro.)
> P. interrupted him. Let him do as he pleased.

Further examples:

> *Ad ogni bivio, alla nostra domanda circa la via da prendere, egli ce ne additava una dicendo che quella era la buona ma che anche l' altra conduceva alla trincea che dovevamo occupare. Scegliessimo.* (Soffici.)

> *Lui serviva chi gli pagava la senseria, e poi non sapeva niente; malignassero i maligni e chiacchierassero i chiacchieroni.* (Bacchelli.)

25

(c) The present and past subjunctives may be used to give a question a surprised or hesitating tone, genuine or ironical ('Can it be that...?', 'Could it be that...?'). In the present or perfect, such a subjunctive must be introduced by *Che*; in the imperfect or pluperfect, it may be introduced by *Che* or *Se*, or again it may stand alone.

> *Che siano venuti?*
> Can they have come?

> *Che t' abbia agguantato te?*
> You don't mean to say he buttonholed **you**?

> *Che la poesia, come ha detto Goethe, sia più vera della verità?*
>   (Papini.)
> Is poetry perhaps, as G. said...?

> *Che avessero poi sbagliato?*
> Could they have been wrong after all?

> *S' egli si fosse ingannato a quel proposito? Se lo aspettassero lunghi anni di una vita simile?* (Fogazzaro.)
> Had he been mistaken about it all? Were there in store for him...?

> *Fosse finita la miniera?* (Pirandello.)
> Surely the mine was not worked out?

> *Nessuno. Fossero fuori?* (Fogazzaro.)
> No one there. Were they outside perhaps?

(d) For the phrase *Fossi matto!* see below, § 37(a).

§ 36. Dependent Subjunctive.

The dependent subjunctive in Italian is very elastically used. In certain cases (e.g. in final clauses) it is of course necessary; in others it is an alternative to the indicative. In these latter cases it is misleading to say that the subjunctive expresses doubt. Certainly, if one wants to express doubt, the subjunctive is the natural mood; but it is often used instead of the indicative merely to put things less strongly, or as a polite understatement—the speaker may have no doubt whatever and yet use the subjunctive to temper an assertion—giving it, one may say, a subjective rather than an objective expression. Thus *credere* is almost always followed by the subjunctive when it refers to the present or past;[1] one says *Credo che sia vero*, however sure one may be.[2] (Cf. the English formula 'I'm **afraid** he's gone away', used even if this is KNOWN to be so.) Again, after PAST tenses of all verbs of saying, supposing[3] and hoping the subjunctive is commoner than the indicative (in written Italian especially); if one really feels doubt, of course one uses the subjunctive; but, apart from this, the subjunctive may merely make a non-committal assertion, in contrast with which the indicative makes a strong assertion. Thus, *Disse che erano venuti, Sperai che sarebbero stati felici* are strong expressions; the commoner formulas *Disse che fossero venuti, Sperai che fossero felici* are merely moderate expressions, by no means suggesting that what the man said was suspect or that my hope was disappointed.[4]

§ 37. Some particular uses of the dependent subjunctive.

(a) In the protasis of a remote conditional ('If he were here. . .'), the imperfect or pluperfect subjunctive is sometimes used without *se* (cf. English 'Were he here. . .').

> *Potessi scegliere, piglierei questo.*
> If I could choose, I should take this.

> *Fosse giunto prima, non sarebbe successa la disgrazia.*
> Had he come earlier, the accident would not have happened.

Such a protasis is sometimes used with the apodosis understood, e.g. *Sapesse!* 'If he only knew!'[5] And this is no doubt the origin of the

---

[1] But it (like *temere*) is normally used with the future and conditional; and it has the present or past indicative (a) in expressions of religious belief; (b) in polite assurances of the kind *Creda che le ho sempre voluto bene.*

[2] *Sono certo* likewise is usually followed by the subjunctive.

[3] I.e. supposing as distinct from reflecting. *Pensava che fossero...*, 'he thought (supposed, believed) that they were...'; *pensava che erano...*, 'he reflected (remembered) that they were...'.

[4] Indeed, if the hope were really disappointed, it would be more idiomatic to use the past conditional, as emphasizing the strength of the hope.

[5] In some contexts, this use shades off into the independent past subjunctive of wish [§ 35(a)].

seemingly independent subjunctive *Fossi matto* (*pazzo*)*!* which is often used in rejecting an offer or supposition, e.g.:

> '*Parla con me.*'
>
> '*Fossi matto! Ho da parlare a lui.*' (Albertini.)
>
> *Ma una mattina lo trovai davanti al dizionario del Petrocchi:—*
> *Tu scriveresti 'orto' per levar del sole?—Io? fossi matto!*
> (Ojetti.)
>
> '*Quanto hai detto che vuoi?*'
>
> '*Venticinque napoleoni.*'
>
> '*Fossi pazzo!*' (Tozzi.)

The English equivalent in conditionals would be an *apodosis*, 'I **should** be a fool (if I did such a thing)'. But the Italian is grammatically a *protasis*—'If I were a fool I might do such a thing'.[1]

(b) The PRESENT subjunctive with *se* or *qualora* is sometimes used in the protasis of a remote conditional when the apodosis is not in the conditional but in the present or future indicative ('If you should doubt my words, you can find the evidence in the book itself').

> *Se alcuno domandi che cosa sieno queste Cronache, la risposta*
> *è meno facile....* (Palmarocchi.)
>
> Should anyone ask what these chronicles are, the answer is less obvious....

This construction is probably commoner with *qualora* than with *se* (*Qualora non ti piaccia, cambierò di progetto*). *Se* itself is often used with the IMPERFECT subjunctive even when the apodosis is present or future, e.g.:

> *Se questa notte—disse il contadino—cominciasse a piovere,*
> *tu puoi andare a cuccia in quel casotto di legno.* (Collodi.)
>
> *Ah! se qualcuno ci tradisse, la pagherà cara.* (Soffici.)

(c) The subjunctive is used in alternative conditionals with single or double *o* ('whether... or...'); there is also a fuller form *o che*.

---

[1] The idiomatic TRANSLATION would of course be something different from either, e.g. 'Nonsense!' or 'What do you take me for?'

Voglia o non voglia, lo dovrà fare. ⎫
Volesse o non volesse, lo dovette fare.⎰

Whether he {likes / liked} it or not, he {will have / had} to do it.[1]

O non capissero o fingessero di non capire, tanto non vollero rispondere.

Whether they didn't understand or just pretended not to, anyhow they wouldn't answer.

Further examples:

Ma vengano in origine dalla natura, o vengano d' altronde, le illusioni allignano nell' animo umano. (Graf.)

I primi canti dell' Inferno sono, in generale, i più gracili; o che appartenessero a un primo abbozzo...o che ritenessero dell' incertezza di tutti i cominciamenti. (Croce.)

Notice the common formula whereby a pair of alternatives is followed by *che dir si voglia* ('whichever you like to call it'), e.g.:

Questa fortuna o sfortuna che dir si voglia.

(d) *Perchè* (='because') takes the subjunctive for a rejected reason, in contrast with the indicative for the true reason.

*Lo feci non perchè **volessi** ma perchè **dovevo**.*
I did it not because I wanted to but because I had to.

*Ma non sempre gli va così. Non perchè l' accollatario... **sia** capace di defraudarlo; ma perchè molte **sono** le cause che possono assottigliargli il guadagno.* (Fucini.)

But it is not always that things go so well with him. Not because (that) the contractor is capable of cheating him, but because there are many causes which go to lessen his profits.

---

[1] Not in such phrases generally, but with *volere* itself in this particular sense, the infinitive may replace the subjunctive: *Volere o non volere* (or *Volere o volare*), *così ha da essere.*

(e) When *come* and *quasi* are used conditionally (i.e. when they stand for *come se, quasi che*) they take the subjunctive.

> *Barcollava come fosse briaco.*
> He was staggering as if he were drunk.

> *Rimasero imperterriti, quasi avessero aspettato il colpo.*
> They were undismayed, as if they had been expecting the blow.

(f) *Benchè, sebbene* and other words meaning 'although' normally take the subjunctive. But the indicative may be used (1) to give emphasis, in any tense; (2) in the future and conditional, to express the time exactly; (3) when 'though' is a connective rather than a conjunction, i.e. when the meaning is 'still, nevertheless', and the clause is felt as independent. Examples:

(1) *...la scuola guelfa che ormai è d' obbligo evocare in certi casi, benchè il paese è officialmente ghibellino.* (Carducci.)

> *Il Leopardi, sebbene fu infelicissimo, non fu però di quegli estremi infelici che....* (Graf.)

(2) *Ma lo Scacerni fida nella propria vigilanza e solerzia per mettersi al riparo...benchè il tratto non sarà breve a scendere.* (Bacchelli.)

> *Benchè in altre condizioni avrebbe fatto a meno di costoro volentieri, non li volle contraddire.* (Bacchelli.)

(3) *Potrai udire gratis un po' di musica; benchè sono anch' io dell' opinione del vostro Caval di spade che bisogna ricondurre la musica italiana al tamburo.* (Fogazzaro.)

> *Di codesto ritrarsi altri potrebbe...trovar la ragione nella caduta d' ogni reggimento democratico.... Sebbene è forse più vero che....* (Carducci.)

> Some might account for this withdrawal thus. **But** it would perhaps be truer to say....

(2) and (3) are quite common uses. (1) should be imitated only with great caution.

(g) Indefinite relatives and conjunctions (*qualunque*,[1] *chiunque*, *dovunque*, etc.) also take the subjunctive normally, but may have the indicative (1) for emphasis, in any tense; (2) to express exact time, in future and conditional. Examples:

(1) *Da qualunque parte si **volge** il piede, la terra ingoia.* (Panzini.)

    *...mettendo le lettere nei gomitoli, nei fazzoletti, nei libri...: insomma, dovunque si **può** nascondere un pezzetto di carta.* (Serao.)

(2) *Qualunque cosa lei **vorrà**, non avrà che chiederla.* (Bontempelli.)

(h) The subjunctive is often used in comparative clauses, where it gives a less positive or a more general sense than the indicative.

    *La risposta è meno facile di quello che **possa** sembrare a prima vista.* (Palmarocchi.)

    *Le labbra di Assunta disegnano, più che non **dicano**, le parole.* (Negri.)

    *Era assai più vero di quanto non **lasciasse** trapelare.* (Bacchelli.)

    *Lasciò le cose d' Italia in peggior condizione di quel che le **avesse** trovate.* (Papini.)

(i) When a noun-clause is reversed (in such formulas as 'That this was so is already known'), the verb in that clause becomes subjunctive (as also in French).

    *Che questo **sia** vero risulta dai documenti* (= *Risulta...che questo **è** vero*).

(j) After *far sì che* ('to bring it about that') the subjunctive is normal. This is worth noting because the corresponding French idiom has the indicative.

---

[1] On *qualunque* it may be noted that, though grammarians consider it purely singular, it has sometimes been used as a plural also. *Qualunque ne fossero le origini e gl' intenti primi....Il mio manifesto politico era ne' miei scritti, qualunque sieno.* Both examples are from Carducci, but scarcely to be imitated. The safe construction is *quali pur fossero (siano)*.

> *Solamente utili sono quelle cose e fatiche le quali arrecando*
> *qualche diletto, fanno sì che gli uomini **scordino** i mali*
> *loro e quasi non **sappian** di vivere.* (Graf.)

(French would say *les choses qui font qu'on n' a guère plus conscience d'être en vie.*)

Tenses of the subjunctive

§ 38. When the context makes the sense clear, the present subjunctive may represent the same TIME as the future indicative, the imperfect subjunctive the same TIME as the conditional. The CHOICE of subjunctive or indicative rests on the principles indicated in § 36.

> *Temo che **venga** domani.*
> I'm afraid he will come to-morrow.
>
> *Suppose che la nonna, rimasta sola, lo **facesse** chiamare.*
> (Fogazzaro.)
> He thought that when his grandmother was alone she would
>   send for him.
>
> *Si credeva che l' ammalato **durasse** qualche ora.* (Fogazzaro.)
> They imagined the patient would last a few hours more.

The subjunctives here make a weaker or more subjective statement than the indicative, though *venga, facesse, durasse* represent the same TIME as *verrà, farebbe, durerebbe*.[1]

Past subjunctives of this kind are common in relative and temporal clauses of oblique or sub-oblique construction. (There is a fluctuation between imperfect and pluperfect subjunctive, corresponding to the fluctuation between present and past conditional, § 14.)

> *I giornali del mattino comunicarono che la polizia regalava*
> *diecimila franchi a chi **avesse ucciso** il leone.* (Angioletti.)
>
> *Gli disse che quando **fosse** pronto, aveva qualcosa da dirgli.*
> (Bacchelli.)

---

[1] Or, in these last two cases, *avrebbe fatto, sarebbe durato.* In RELATIVE or ADVERBIAL clauses the pluperfect subjunctive may replace the past conditional (see the later examples here); it could not be used in these two clauses, for obvious reasons of sense.

*Dissero...che quando le sue occupazioni gliene **avessero lasciato** il tempo, sarebbero stati lietissimi di riceverlo.* (Verga.)

*Ah, quando l' Italia **fosse** libera, come la servirebbe!* (Fogazzaro.)

(This use of tenses may not seem noticeable because in similar clauses English uses a present for direct speech and a simple past for indirect: 'We offer a reward to anyone who **kills**', 'They offered a reward to anyone who **killed**'; 'When you **are** ready...', 'He said that when he **was** ready...'. But according to Italian convention [§ 4(b)] the tenses of direct speech would be future or future perfect:

*A chi **avrà** ucciso, Quando **sarai** pronto, Quando le sue occupazioni gliene **avranno lasciato**..., Quando l' Italia **sarà** libera.*)

Contrast:

*Rimise ogni decisione a più tardi, quando **avrebbe parlato** a sua moglie.* (Fogazzaro.)

Here the conditional makes the point more positively than *avesse parlato* would have done.

§ **39.** Periphrastic subjunctive.

We have seen already (1) that the rules for the subjunctive may be relaxed in favour of future and conditional [§ 36, n. 1 and § 37(f) and (g)]; and (2) that present and past subjunctives may in fact represent the future and conditional (§ 38). Thus if we wish to say 'I'm afraid he will come', 'Whoever it is going to be', we already have the choice of (1) *Temo che **verrà**, Chiunque **sarà**;* (2) *Temo che **venga**, Chiunque **sia**.* But an author may wish to use the subjunctive in such a case (for the sake of strictness or to keep a subjective tone) and yet to indicate the time more exactly than the present or imperfect allows. He may then resort to the **periphrastic subjunctive,** i.e. he may use the present or imperfect subjunctive of one of three verbs of future meaning—*avere a, essere (stare) per, dovere*—followed by the infinitive. Such periphrasis may be used in several kinds of clause, but is common only with expressions of fear; and *avere a*[1] is the most frequent periphrastic verb.

> *Le rondini gridano impazzite dallo spavento che il gran miracolo dell' aurora non **abbia a tornare** più mai* ('the fear that dawn will never return'). (Ojetti.)

> *Avevan temuto che quella morte…non **avesse a avvelenare** le carni* ('might OR would poison the meat'). (Bacchelli.)

> *Impensieriti che quella stagionaccia…**avesse a sciupare** [il giorno della festa].* (Fucini.)

> *Io penso che, quando sia giunto il tempo di cogliere il frutto, questo non **abbia a corrispondere** a così lungo ed aspro tormento di studi.* (Panzini.)

> *Quando nessuno crede più che **abbiano a finire*** ('that they will ever come to an end'). (Bacchelli.)

> *Speravano…che la burrasca **fosse per cacciare** la selvaggina verso il piano.* (Bacchelli.)

> *Nessuno di noi dubita ormai che, qualunque sia **per essere** lo sforzo necessario, al momento stabilito c' impadroniremo di quella trincea.* (Soffici.)

[Cf. also Ojetti's sentence quoted in § 83(b), (iii).]

The imperative

§ 40. There is an idiomatic use of the imperative which stands outside strict syntax. The second singular imperative (usually repeated, and often reinforced by the prefix *ri-*) is used to express prolonged or repeated effort. Most frequently, but not always, the action belongs to the subject of the sentence. There is no consistent English equivalent, but examples should make the idiom clear.

> *Prova riprova non ne indovinò mai una.*
> Try as he would, he could never get anything right.

---

[1] A good example of this in the indicative is in Bacchelli's sentence: *Una sera o l' altra, qualche bastone gli aveva ad accarezzar le spalle* ('He was likely to get set upon and beaten'). Distinguish this sense from that of 'having occasion to', e.g. *Come già ebbe a notare il Manzoni* ('as M. once had occasion to observe').

34

Cerca ricerca lo trovammo lì.
After a long search we found it there.

Batti oggi e batti domani, il farmacista ha strappato final-
mente al dottor Calajò la promessa.... (Pirandello.)
Hammering away day in day out, the chemist at last extracts
the promise....

Lo scartafaccio che, prega e riprega, egli mi mostrò. (Ojetti.)
The notebook he showed me after many requests.

Further examples:

Cammina cammina essi arrivarono prima che fosse notte.
(Deledda.)

Tasta e ritasta, dài picchia e mena, qualche cosa entrò
nella mente a Beppino. (Cicognani.)

Spingi da una banda e tira dall' altra, mi faceva (=facevo)
strada fra quella boscaglia natante. (Nievo.)

I due bravi professori inglesi, gira e rigira intorno all' apparta-
mento del Blake, l' usciolo segreto non eran riusciti a
trovarlo. (Praz.)

Substitutes for *essere*

§ 41. There are certain verbs which often replace *essere*: (a) in
forming the passive (or the quasi-passive of certain verbs); (b) with
an adjective-predicate. These are (a) *venire* in simple tenses and
rimanere, restare, andare in simple and compound tenses; (b) *riuscire,
tornare, risultare.*

Venire is the most general substitute for *essere* in the passive.
Typical examples are: *Venne sfrattato*, 'He was (OR got) dismissed';
Mi vien detto, 'I am told'; *Le lettere gli venivan date*, 'The letters
were always given him'.

(The phrase *vien fatto a uno (di...)* has various shades of meaning
lying between 'succeed', 'manage', 'be able'. *Gli venne fatto
d' imparare...*, 'He succeeded in learning'; *Se ti vien fatto questo, me
ne rallegrerò tanto*, 'If you manage to do it I shall be delighted';

In cima al monte, veniva fatto di scorgere le tre frontiere, 'At the top of the mountain one could pick out the three frontiers'.)[1]

Rimanere is chiefly used (1) with verbs of emotion, especially surprise; (2) with verbs of hurting and killing. Thus we frequently have (1) *Rimase sconcertato, meravigliato, spaventato, stupito, allibito;*[2] (2) *Rimasero feriti, uccisi.* Note that in translation it would be quite wrong to say, e.g. 'He **remained** bewildered', 'They **remained** wounded'. 'He **was** bewildered (wounded)' would be the ordinary equivalent, but sometimes it might be worth while to say 'He **was left** bewildered (wounded)'.

(Akin to these uses of *rimanere* with participle are the absolute uses: (1) *Rimase male,* 'He was shocked' or 'He was taken aback'; and *Rimase* alone, 'He was astonished' or 'This was a shock to him'; (2) in some contexts, *Ci rimasero* or merely *Rimasero,* 'They were killed'.)

Restare is used in much the same way as *rimanere,* e.g. *Restò sbalordito, Restò ferito*; but it is rather less common. It is also used absolutely as a strong word of surprise, e.g. in stage directions: GIULIO (*restando*)—*Ma...* [=GIULIO (*surprised*)—'But...'].

Andare with past participle most often indicates obligation, and this is very common indeed in the present tense, e.g. *Questo va fatto,* 'This must be done'. But it is untrue to say, as Grandgent for instance does ('Italian Grammar', p. 49), that *andare* with past participle 'always' implies duty or obligation. It is also used as a mere passive (1) with verbs of praise or blame, *Va lodato, Va biasimato,* though this is now somewhat archaic; (2) with verbs of losing, wasting, destroying, etc. This latter is a good current use, e.g.:

> *Faresti una buona azione, che non **vanno mai perse.*** (Bacchelli.)
> You would be doing a good action, and they are never wasted.

---

[1] *Vien fatto* has also the sense of 'it happens to one', 'one finds oneself...', e.g. *Mi venne fatto di pensare,* 'I happened to think' or 'I found myself thinking'. But this may be more neatly expressed by *viene di...* without *fatto,* e.g. *Gli venne di piangere,* 'He found himself weeping', 'He was overcome by tears'. Distinguish this from *Gli venne da piangere,* 'He felt like weeping'.

[2] Note that the first three participles are truly passive, since *sconcertare, meravigliare, spaventare* are transitive verbs; the last two are what I have called quasi-passive, since *stupire* and *allibire* are intransitive.

*Mezza giornata **andrà perduta**.* (Pirandello.)
Half the day will be wasted.

*Perchè i suoi beni non **andassero divisi*** ('should not be split up'). (Deledda.)

*Tutti i lavori...**andrebbero distrutti*** ('would be destroyed'). (Bacchelli.)

*È a lamentare che **sieno andati perduti*** ('there have been lost') *certi pensieri del Monti intorno all' 'Ortis.'* (Graf.)

Andare may also replace *essere* with certain adjectives, e.g. *andar superbo di*, 'to be proud of'; *andar soggetto ai raffreddori*, 'to be subject to colds'; *andar pazzo* (or *matto*) *per* (or *di*), 'to be mad on, have a passion for'. It is roughly equivalent to *diventare* in: *andare sposa a*, 'to be married to'; *andar soldato*, 'to enlist'.

§ 42. *Riuscire, tornare, risultare* are all (in a proper context) good translations for **be** in the sense of **prove**, e.g. when an action **is** or **proves** easy, hard, impossible, acceptable, unexpected. *Riesce chiaro; gli tornò facile; risultò inattuabile.*

> *Quando [Manzoni] analizza, riesce sempre ammirabile.* (De Sanctis.)
>
> *Era stata sempre fedele alla massima che nella vita tutto torna utile.* (Lisi.)

§ 43. One further idiom may here be mentioned—an occasional substitute for *essere* from the translator's rather than the grammarian's point of view. This is the impersonal 3rd PLURAL, as in *Dicono*, 'they say', 'it is said'. In this instance the Italian idiom may be paralleled in English. But it is also used more widely, as in *Picchiarono alla porta* (Ojetti), *Ella trasalì come se avessero sorpreso il suo segreto* (Fogazzaro), where the original context in either case shows that only one person could be concerned. For the translator, then, this is one possible way of turning 'There **was** a knock at the door', 'As if her secret **had been** found out'.

37

Cases following certain verbs

§ **44**. Dictionaries and grammars fail to make it clear that certain verbs may take either an indirect or a direct object. The following list covers the commonest cases:

> To fulfil a duty. *Adempiere* (*adempire*) *un dovere* or *a un dovere*.
>
> They helped her. *La soccorsero, la sovvennero* or *Le soccorsero, le sovvennero*.
>
> I assured him that.... *Gli assicurai* or *Lo assicurai che*....
>
> He is like his brother. *Somiglia* (*rassomiglia*) *il fratello* or *al fratello*.
>
> It did not interest him. *Non gli interessava* or *Non lo interessava*.
>
> They forgave her. *Le perdonarono* or *La perdonarono*.
>
> It bored them all. *Li seccava tutti* or *Seccava a tutti*.
>
> To serve a master. *Servire un padrone* or *a un padrone*.
>
> To obey the king. *Obbedire al re* or *il re*.

Pensare, 'to think of', has usually an indirect object, but may have a direct one in a rather stronger sense. *Penso a lui* (never *gli penso*), 'I turn my thoughts to him, he comes into my mind'; *Lo penso*, 'My thoughts are full of him, he occupies my mind'. Fogazzaro is specially fond of this second use, e.g. *Camminava adagio, pensando Velo..., pensando Leila e non volendo pensarla*.

Strappare ('to snatch, tear', or 'rescue FROM') is followed by *a*: (1) for persons, always; (2) for things, when the sense is metaphorical. It is followed by *da* for things when the sense is literal.

> They rescued the boy **from** his tormentors.
> *Strapparono il ragazzo **ai** suoi tormentatori.*
>
> He was torn away **from** his contemplation, his studies, etc.
> *Venne strappato **alla** contemplazione, **agli** studi, ecc.*
>
> I tore the book **from** his hands.
> *Gli strappai il libro **dalle** mani.*

Idioms of the impersonal reflexive

§ **45**. In the sense of an English 3rd plural passive, e.g. 'Such things are never (have never been) seen'. Here, instead of the ordinary personal reflexive, *Non si vedono (si sono viste) mai cose simili*, one may use the impersonal reflexive form *Non si vede (si è visto) mai cose simili*. But in this case the subject must follow the verb; if we begin with *Cose simili*, we must continue with *non si vedono*.

N.B. Obviously such a phrase as *Si vede queste cose* approaches the sense of '*One sees* these things', i.e. *queste cose* looks more like an object than a subject. Hence some writers use a construction where *si* is treated as an impersonal subject and an accusative pronoun is added before it, e.g. *Lo si vede*, 'It is seen', *Ci si loda*, 'We are praised'. Purists stigmatize this construction as barbarous, and certainly it is better left alone. But everyone allows *La si loda*, 'she is praised', because *la* is or may be a true nominative, the short form of *ella*; the corresponding plural is *le si lodano*.

§ **46**. In the sense of an English verb (usually intransitive or copulative) with such indefinite subjects as 'one', 'people', 'they', 'you', etc.

(a) If a verb so used is normally compounded with *essere*, any predicate or participle becomes plural.

> *Quando si è giovani.* When one is young.
>
> *Si diventava inquieti.* They were getting restless.
>
> *Più sciocchi di così si muore.* (Literally, 'If you are stupider than this, you die'; idiomatic for 'This is the last word in stupidity'.)
>
> *Si era partiti* (= *Erano partiti*) *a mezzanotte.* They had all left (the party had left) at midnight.

N.B. Such a plural predicate is also normal with an infinitive, e.g. *È difficile esser giusti in causa sua*, 'It is hard to be just in one's own cause'.[1]

---

[1] Further examples of this. *Esser famosi significa diventare, insieme, vecchi e perseguitati.* (Papini.) '*Sei un disperato.*' '*Per non esserlo, bisognerebbe essere o stupidi o corrotti.*' (Bacchelli.)

(b) If a verb so used is normally compounded with *avere*, the participle is unchanged.

> *Si è dormito* (= **Hanno** *dormito*) *bene*. They have all slept well.
>
> *Se ne era parlato in città*. People in town had talked about it.

(c) If a verb already reflexive is to be given an impersonal sense, this construction does not suffice. Thus *Si sveglia* cannot mean 'One wakes', to express which we must say *Uno si sveglia* or *Ci si sveglia* [see § 47(b)].

§ 47. After *noi*.

(a) There is a Tuscan idiom by which one says, e.g. *Noi si crede*, *Noi si è stanchi*, for *Crediamo, Siamo stanchi*. *Noi* here may be used either in the strict personal sense of 'we', or in the wider sense 'men of our time', 'people like us', which may be called impersonal. This reflexive form often alternates with the ordinary form. Thus Papini has *Noi altri si levò di mezzo il letto*[1] ('We cleared away the bed') and, just after, *Noi altri portammo*.... If the context makes the sense clear, *noi* may be omitted or may be replaced by *tutti*.

Further examples:

> *Noi italiani s' è tanto placidi*. (Ojetti.)
>
> *Tutti s' andava* ('We all went'). (Papini.)
>
> *Finito il concerto, s' è rimasti* ('we stayed') *con Toscanini*. (Ojetti.)
>
> *Se volete che noi stessi vi* (indirect object) *si doni il fiore del nostro spirito*.... (Angioletti.)
>
> *Si passò tutti insieme una bella mezz' ora*. (Cecchi.)
>
> *Si fu introdotti da un servitore*. (Papini.)

(b) When the verb to be used is already reflexive, *ci* as direct object is added before *si*, and *noi* is usually dropped, e.g. *Ci si accorge* (= *Ci accorgiamo*, 'We observe'). It must be understood that *ci* as direct object should be strictly reflexive or reciprocal, not a substitute

---

Note that although in this construction the verb may be followed by a noun or disjunctive pronoun as direct object (*Noi si vede lui solo*), *ci* is the only direct pronoun-object which may precede.

for the passive; e.g. *Ci si ama* should have the sense of 'We love ourselves' or 'We love each other', never the sense 'We are loved'.[1] (Cf. § 45.) But of course one may say *Ci si vuol bene* for 'We are loved', because *Ci* there is indirect.

Here as in (a), the special form often alternates with the ordinary form; e.g. Albertini has *ci si destava* followed by *ci riunivamo*.

Further examples:

> *Allora per mesi ci si burlò del ministro.* (Ojetti.)
>
> *Qualche volta ci s' imbatteva in un prete.* (Papini.)
>
> *Noi si scivola sull' acqua e ci si alza felici.* (Ojetti.)

[1] This in deference to the strong feelings of Tuscan grammarians on the subject. Fogazzaro, Ojetti, Pirandello use the forbidden construction.

II

NOUNS

Gender

§ 48. The student should beware of transferring French genders to Italian. The following examples are given *à titre d'indication*.

ITALIAN	FRENCH
Un allarme	*Une alarme*
Un' appendice	*Un appendice*
Un' arte	*Un art*
La calma	*Le calme*
La carrozza	*Le carrosse*
La corrente	*Le courant*
Il costume (custom or costume)	{ *La coutume* (custom) { *Le costume* (costume)
Il dente	*La dent*
La diocesi	*Le diocèse*
Un enimma	*Une énigme*
Il fiore[1]	*La fleur*
Il flauto	*La flûte*
La fronte normally; rarely *Il fronte* [*letterario e assai pedantesco* (Petrocchi); but allowable in the military sense]	*Le front*
Un idolo	*Une idole*
{ *Un intrigo* (intrigue) { *Un intreccio* (plot of a book)	*Une intrigue*
Una lega (alloy, quality, e.g. *di buona lega*)	*Un aloi* (*de bon aloi*
Il limite	*La limite*
Il mare	*La mer*

[1] ALL Italian nouns ending in accented *-óre* are masculine.

42

ITALIAN	FRENCH
Il margine (rarely *La margine* in sense of 'scar')	*La marge*
La mattina (commoner) or *Il mattino* (strictly, 'early morning')	*Le matin*
Il metodo	*La méthode*
Il periodo	*La période*
Il pianeta[1]	*La planète*
⎰*La piega* (fold, bend, turn) ⎱*Il plico* (bundle of papers)	*Le pli*
Il tentativo	*La tentative*

Diminutives and augmentatives

§ 49. Useful examples of the various forms of suffix are to be found (a) in Hoare's 'Dictionary', under *Donna* and *Donnona*; (b) in the two relevant chapters of '*L' idioma gentile*' by De Amicis. Such simple suffixes as *-ino*, *-one*, *-accio* may be used fairly freely; the more picturesque or elaborate forms (e.g. *Borghettaccio, ragazzettuccio*) are better avoided unless one has seen or heard them used in a context precisely similar.

Note that the use of the diminutive is in some cases obligatory and in others customary. Thus an electric bell is always a *campanello*, not a *campana* ('church bell'); the window of a railway-carriage or car is a *finestrino*, not a *finestra*; and an ordinary restaurant-table or working-table is a *tavolino*, not a *tavola*.[2] Again, babies are usually said to have *manine* and *piedini*, and the heroines of some novels share the privilege.

Adoptive nouns

§ 50. In theory, any part of speech in Italian may become a noun by having an article or demonstrative prefixed. This is particularly common with adverbs; *il come, il quando* are probably used more freely in Italian than 'the how', 'the when' in English. Commonest

---

[1] *La pianeta* is a quite different word meaning 'chasuble'.
[2] But *il tavolo* is sometimes used in the same sense as *il tavolino*.

of all is *il perchè* ('the reason' rather than 'the why'); thus one may write: *questo povero perchè*, 'this pathetic reason'; *tutti questi perchè*, 'all these reasons'; *un perchè qualunque*, 'a reason of any kind'.

Adverbial objective case

§ 51. Modern Italian still allows at times the once common idiom of the adverbial objective case—that is, the use of a noun (grammatically in the objective) after an adjective or participle. The type is *pallido la faccia* ('white in face, white of face, white-faced'). It is a distinctly literary use. Examples:

> *Curva il capo.* (D' Annunzio.)
>
> *Jeanne camminava a caso, legata i pensieri e i sensi alla presenza di Maironi.* (Fogazzaro.)
>
> *Carica le braccia d' erbe e di stoviglie, una ragazza. . . .* (Cecchi.)
>
> *Le placide bestie ruminanti, bianche le vaste schiene e i tepidi fianchi.* (Bacchelli.)
>
> *Il Petrarca, tutto pieno l' anima e l' ingegno della poesia latina.* (Carducci.)
>
> *Ella lo guardò, soffusa il viso di un lieve rossore.* (Fogazzaro.)

Collective noun-endings

§ 52. Notice the endings *-aglia, -ame, -ume*, which may all be collective: *la nuvolaglia*, 'the mass of clouds'; *il contadiname*, 'the peasantry'; *il sudiciume*, 'the mass of dirt'. The first two forms are often contemptuous (*canaglia, servitorame*) but often again are not so at all; *-ume* is nearly always contemptuous, and as applied to a crowd of persons is very rude indeed (e.g. *inglesume* would mean 'English scum').

Plural for singular

§ 53. Italian often has plural nouns where we have singular. 'He makes good progress', *fa bei progressi*; 'in my reading', *nelle mie letture*; 'your health', *le tue condizioni di salute*; 'this information', *queste informazioni*.

44

III

PRONOUNS AND PRONOMINAL ADJECTIVES

Insertion or omission of pronouns

§ 54. Italian is not so strict as French in inserting pronouns implied by the sense. If one takes as example the sentence 'He looks rich but he isn't', French idiom makes it necessary to say *mais il ne l'est pas*; in Italian one may say either *ma non lo è* or merely *ma non è*.

Examples of omission:

> *O siamo dominatori o non siamo.* (Papini.)
>
> *Pareva vecchia ma non era.* (Pirandello.)
>
> *Avrebbe voluto pensarci, e non poteva.* (Fogazzaro.)
>
> *Egli è sempre tormentato dal desiderio di divertirsi, e non può, non deve.* (Serao.)

Examples of insertion:

> *La coltura oggi non è più ereditaria di quel che non lo sia l' ingegno e il coraggio.* (Bacchelli.)
>
> *Era poi davvero sua madre, quella? E se lo era?* (Deledda.)

When two reflexive verbs follow each other immediately, the second reflexive pronoun is sometimes dropped.

> *Si vestiva e spogliava da sola.* (Bontempelli.)
>
> *...s' innovasse e perfezionasse.* (Carducci.)

Particular pronouns and pronominal adjectives

§ 55. *Esso* as a demonstrative. *Esso* may and should sometimes be used as a substitute for *questo*, when (a) the noun it goes with refers to things not persons, and (b) the noun has been used already, so that 'this' has the sense of 'the aforesaid' or 'such', e.g.:

> *Parlò a lungo delle regole d' arte, benchè di esse regole poco si curasse lavorando.*
>
> He talked a great deal about the rules of art, though in his own work he bothered little about these (such) rules.

§ 56. *Quello.*

(a) Form of the masculine plural. It is best for the student to keep to the grammar-book rule of using *quegli*, not *quelli*, before vowels or *s* impure, e.g. *quegli stessi*, *quegli occhi*. Nevertheless, some good authors write *quelli stessi*, *quelli occhi* (a practice quite justified both historically and phonetically).[1]

(b) *Quello* for English article. It is customary in Italian to use *quello* rather than *il* with an adjective whose noun is understood, e.g. 'I prefer old books to new', *Preferisco i libri vecchi a quelli nuovi.*

> *Molte delle colonne sono quelle antiche* ('the old ones') *della piscina romana.* (Ojetti.)
>
> *...entrato da un orecchio e uscito di quell' altro.* (Cicognani.)

But the article is sometimes used as in English.

> *Altro suono non era nell' aria che il fioco della Riderella e il profondo del Posina.* (Fogazzaro.)

(c) Note the idioms: *In quel di Firenze*, 'in Florentine territory'; *è sempre quello*, 'he hasn't changed'; *non è più quello di prima*, 'he's not what he once was'; *in quella*, 'at that point (moment)'.

§ 57. Attraction of *quello* as antecedent.

In phrases of the kind 'what is (are) called so-and-so', *quello* used as antecedent may be attracted into the gender and number of the predicate.

(a) When the verb in the relative clause is *chiamarsi* or its equivalent, this is the normal construction, e.g. 'what is called stupidity', *quella che si chiama (si dice) stoltezza.*

---

[1] Similarly, some good authors prefer *belli occhi* to the usual *begli occhi*.

*Dopo **quella** che lui chiamò **colazione**.* (Fucini.)

*La superstizione di **quella** che si dice **civiltà**.* (Panzini.)

*Non ho mai avuto **quelle** che si chiamano **crisi** d' anima.* (Papini.)

*[L' arte vera] diffida in sommo grado di **quelli** che diconsi **ornamenti**.* (Graf.)

But *quel(lo) che* is also possible, e.g.:

*...perdere **quel** che oggi si dicono **i diritti civili**.* (Papini.)

(b) The attraction is also fairly common when *essere* is the verb, e.g.:

*In lui pareva sprezzo anche **quella** ch' era magari soltanto **noia**.* (Bacchelli.)

But the unattracted form is at least equally common here, e.g.:

***Quel** che fu e doveva essere **la fondamentale esigenza**....* (Bacchelli.)

(c) With other verbs attraction is possible but exceptional.

***Quella** che mi manca è **la voglia**.* (Borgese.)

***Quella** che per le vie...s' addensa, tumultua e ondeggia...non è più **folla**, è **massa** di popolo.* (Manacorda.)

§ 58. A similar attraction is found in the Tuscan phrases: *quella po' po' di tempesta* (Fucini), *questa po' di fatica* (Papini), *Que' po' po' di cenci che avevano addosso* (Fucini). *Poco* in itself is of course masculine singular.

59. Ellipse and attraction with possessives.

Possessives are often used in Italian with what seems to us an ellipse, e.g.:

Era amore il suo? (Albertini.)

In English this needs to be amplified, e.g. 'Was his feeling love?' or 'Was it love that he felt?'

Such ellipse is accompanied by attraction, e.g.:

Non era ambizione la mia. (Papini.)

What possessed me was not ambition.

Più che una partenza, la sua è una fuga. (Manacorda.)
His action is less a leave-taking than a flight.[1]

Non erano discorsi i suoi; erano cascate, frane, diluvi di parole.
(De Amicis.)
His utterances were not speeches....

*La nostra in cui viviamo si potrebbe chiamare più ignoranza che
corruzione.* (Bacchelli.)
The condition we live in might be called ignorance rather than
corruption.

§ 60. Gender of *qualche cosa*. As is well known, when *qualche cosa*
is followed by *di* and an adjective, the adjective is masculine, e.g.
qualche cosa di buono. What if there is no *di*? Adjectives or participles
which follow may be either masculine or feminine.

Masculine. *Un qualche cosa a lei sconosciuto.* (Bonsanti.)

Feminine. *Qualche cosa era accaduta.* (Pirandello.)
C' era in me qualche cosa che non era schiava. (Albertini.)

But an adjective coming between *qualche* and *cosa* must of course be
feminine: *qualche altra cosa, qualche nuova cosa*.

§ 61. Relative *chi*. It is an elementary rule that relative *chi* is not
a substitute for *che*; it means *colui che*, 'he who, one who, the man
who'. But it is to be observed that *chi* is more widely used than its
literal English equivalents. 'He who' now belongs to the language of
proverbs ('He who hesitates is lost'), and we do not very often say
'one who' or 'the man who'. But Italian constantly uses *chi* with
a verb where we should merely use a noun, e.g. *chi scrive* for 'a writer'
or 'writers'; this is probably an inheritance from classical Latin.

Ma chi conduce l' automobile pensa mai a Volta o a Ferraris?
(Ojetti.)
But does a car-driver ever think of V. or F.?

Questo disdoro inquieto chi lo ammirava.
This disgrace alarmed his admirers.

---

[1] On a further difference of English and Italian idiom here see § 82.

A chi legge.
To the reader

Affidandosi all' onestà di chi comprava. (Deledda.)
Trusting the decency of the customer.

N.B. As is clear from these examples, *chi* so used sometimes corresponds to an English singular, sometimes to a plural; but in either case it takes a singular verb (unless, of course, it is object not subject in its own clause, which happens rarely: *Io non sono chi credono*, 'I am not the man they take me for').

§ 62. Relative *quanto, quanti.* These are used in much the same way as *chi*, but chiefly after prepositions. *Quanto* of course is singular and refers to things, *quanti* is plural and refers to persons.

A quanto si vede.
Judging by appearances.

Dopo quanto avevano detto.
After all their statements.

Fuor della vista di quanti ballavano.
Out of sight of the dancers.

Note in the following example the alternation of *quanti* with plural verb and *chi* with singular (the SENSE is plural in either case):

> ...*alienando gli animi di quanti avevano sperato riforme, incrudendoli in chi voleva rivoluzione.* (Bacchelli.)

§ 63. Relative *chi* with subjunctive. *Chi* with subjunctive is sometimes used in a conditional sense: 'If one....'

> *Quanta saviezza, chi la sapesse cercare* ('if one only knew how to look for it'), *v' è nella letteratura popolare burlesca!* (Papini.)

> *La quale, chi la consideri com' era in effetto nel secolo decimoquarto...* ('Italy, if one considers her as she really was...'). (Carducci.)

64. *Quale.*

(a) Relative *quale* is often used by itself in the sense of *tale...
quale*; as object, it may have a conjunctive pronoun doubling it.

> *Io **quale** mi vedete.*
>
> *La mattina dopo fu sorpreso di vedere che il mondo era **quale**
> doveva essere.* (Borgese.)
>
> *Anche se il risultato non è **quale** vorresti....* (Albertini.)
>
> *Se la condizione dell' Italia non fosse **quale** egli la vien
> descrivendo nelle sue lettere....* (Graf.)

(b) *Quale* may be used elliptically in comparisons where *come*
would also stand. 'He fought like a lion', *Combattè **quale** un leone*
(where French, contrariwise, might say *tel un lion*).

§ **65.** *Altro.* Notice some idiomatic uses.

> *Non è da farci altro.* There's nothing for it.
>
> *Senz' altro.* Without more ado.
>
> *Non ci mancherebbe altro.* It's the last straw.

In conversation, *Altro!* as a reply means 'So-and-so isn't the word
for it!', and hence is a strong affirmative.

> *Ti sei divertito? — Altro!*
>
> 'Did you have a good time?' 'I should think I did!'

Altro che! is often used in the same way.[1] On the other hand,
Tutt' altro! is a strong negative—'Far from it!'

> '*Sei peso dimolto?*'
>
> '*Peso? tutt' altro! Son leggiero come una foglia.*' (Collodi.)
>
> 'Are you very heavy?'
>
> 'Heavy? Far from it! I'm as light as a feather.'
>
> *Cerca tutt' altro che di prendere moglie.*
>
> He is far from intending to get married.

---

[1] But sometimes (at least when the phrase just used is actually repeated),
Altro che may have a corrective or even a strong negative sense. *E i miei
compagni sono pronti? Altro che pronti!* ('Ready indeed!'). *Son partiti due
ore fa.* (Collodi.) *Altro che guarigione! Forse stava peggio; anzi, certo stava
peggio.* (Albertini.)

IV

ADVERBS

§ 66. *Più (non più)*.

(a) In many sentences *non...più* is the equivalent of 'not... again', 'not...now', etc. (instead of 'no longer', 'no more').

> *Da quel giorno in poi non l' abbiamo più visto.*
> Since then we have never seen him again.

> *Non si sposeranno più.*
> The marriage will not now take place.

> *Non avendolo fatto subito, non lo fece più.* (Albertini.)
> Having failed to do it at once, he did not do it afterwards.

(b) *Più* is sometimes combined with *poco* instead of with a direct negative; the sense is then 'little...now', 'little...left', etc.

> *Ce n' è poco più, e glielo voglio far sentire.* (Panzini.)
> There's only a little left, and I want you to taste it.

> *A prima vista si direbbe che in Italia abbiamo più pochi monumenti dell' imponenza di questi.* (Ojetti.)
> At first sight one would say that we have few monuments left in Italy so impressive as these.

> *Della scoltura le importava più poco.* (Bacchelli.)
> She cared little for sculpture now.

§ 67. *Poi*. An idiomatic sense of *poi* is 'after all', e.g. *Se dovesti spendere anche cento lire, non sarebbe **poi** il finimondo.*

> *Prima d' informarla voglio accertarmi che non si tratti **poi** di un' impostura.* (Fogazzaro.)
> Before I tell her I want to make sure that it isn't a hoax after all.

4-2

68. *Fino* (*fin*, *sino*, *sin*) is used adverbially in the sense of 'even', when it is rather stronger than *anche*.

> *Evitava di parlargli e fin di vederlo.* (Bontempelli.)

> *Un Dante che guata con cipiglio michelangiolesco i grandi della terra e fino i santi del cielo.* (Papini.)

The compounds *perfino* (*persino*) and *finanche* are stronger still.
> *A volte dimenticava persino di mangiare.* (Angioletti.)

§ 69. *Pure.*

Pure (*pur*) has many senses. The most important are as follows:

(a) *Pure* = 'also, too'. Most used with pronouns, e.g. *Venne lui pure*, 'he came too'.

(b) *Pure* = 'nevertheless'. *Egli è il meno reo, pure paga per tutti.* (De Sanctis.) But this sense is no longer common except in the compound *e pure* (*eppure*) and after relative *che*, e.g. *La parte di verità che pur c' era nelle parole di Olimpia* (Bacchelli).

(c) *Pure* = 'even'. *Pioppi...così palpitanti pur nell' aria senza vento.* (Panzini.) *La vita, pur con le sue fatiche e i suoi dolori, è più desiderabile della morte.* (Della Seta.)

(d) *Pure* as an emphatic particle, not translatable by any single word: *Credilo pure* ('**Do** believe it'); *Udite pure* ('**Just** listen'); *Andiamo a piedi? — Andiamo pure* ('Shall we walk?' 'Yes, let's'). *Faccia pure* is used as a polite form of permission to anyone to go on doing whatever he is doing ('Please go on', 'Don't mind me'— seriously or ironically). It is sometimes used elliptically. For instance, a customer enters a café and finds a waiter elaborately clearing a table. The waiter says *Vengo subito, signore* ('I'll come in a moment, sir') and the customer replies *Faccia pure*, which does not mean 'Do come', but 'Do go on with your clearing' and so 'Take your time' or 'No hurry'.

§ 70. Compounds of *pure.*

(a) *Se pure* (*seppure*) = (1) if indeed, (2) even if. (1) may be used elliptically, e.g. *Aveva vent' anni, se pure*, 'He was only twenty, if that'.

(b) *Purtroppo* originally = 'only too truly', then 'unfortunately'.

(c) *Pur di* with infinitive, used of the subject of the sentence = *purchè* with subjunctive, 'provided that', 'as long as', or often 'just to'.

> *S' agitava, pronta a tutto **pur d'** impedire una scena violenta.* (Deledda.)
> ...Ready to do anything as long as she could prevent....

> *Una ditta di Milano affrontava il fallimento **pur di** battere tutti i concorrenti.* (Angioletti.)
> A Milanese firm risked bankruptcy just to beat all competitors.

§ 71. *Neppure*, etc.

Neppure, neanche, nemmeno[1] all mean 'not even', and their ordinary usage requires no explanation. The following points are more idiomatic.

(a) *Neppure*, etc. may mean 'less than', in reference to time or place.

> *Neanche in otto giorni.*
> In less than a week.

> *Fra neppure quattro miglia.*
> In less than four miles (OR In under four miles).

(b) *Neppure*, etc. may be combined with the conditional forms lacking *se* [§ 37 (a)].

> *Neanche potessi....*   Not even if I could.
> *Nemmeno fosse più ricco del doppio....* (Bacchelli.)
> Not even if he had been twice as rich.

(c) *E neppure* = 'nor even'.
> *Non è metodo inglese, nè tedesco, nè francese **e neppure** italiano.* (De Sanctis.)

(d) There are also various elliptical usages, of which the commonest is *Neanche a farlo apposta*. This means in origin 'Not even if it had been done (arranged) on purpose (could something have

---

[1] With the rarer forms *neanco* and *nemmanco*.

been more so—the weather hotter, the food worse, etc.)'. The phrase is now a vague adverbial superlative, e.g.:

> *Ella prese una vettura per arrivare più presto; ma **neppure a farlo apposta** il cavallo sdrucciolava...e il vetturino... lo faceva camminare piano.* (Deledda.)

> She took a cab to get there quicker, but the horse kept slipping and the driver kept him down to a walking pace. **It could not possibly have been worse.** [Or one might perhaps say 'the horse kept slipping **as if to spite her**'.][1]

There are other ellipses in the following:

> *Gli si scagliò addosso, che **neanche** un leone.* (Pirandello.)

> He went for him like a lion. [Literally, 'in such a way that not even a lion...'. For *che*, see § 80(b).]

> *Lo diceva con un tono per cui l' avvocato la guardava a occhi spalancati: **neanche** se egli le avesse data una buona notizia!* (Cicognani.)

> The lawyer has announced bad news to the woman and is amazed at her buoyancy. The sentence might be filled out 'Not even if he had given her good news could she have spoken more cheerfully'. The idiomatic equivalent would be something like 'Why, it might have been good news he had announced'.

§ 72. *Giù, su, via.*

English often prefers to express different kinds of motion not by different verbs but by the simple verbs 'go' and 'come' followed by appropriate adverbs. Thus we usually say 'go up', 'come down', 'go away' rather than 'ascend', 'descend', 'depart'. In French, generally speaking, one must use separate verbs. Italian has the choice of either method.

---

[1] To make this idiom obscurer still, *neanche* itself is sometimes dropped (see Hoare, under *Apposta*); but I should say that some negative is always felt to be in the background.

ENGLISH	FRENCH	ITALIAN
Go up	*Monter*	{ *Andar su* *Salire (montare)*
Come down	*Descendre*	{ *Venir giù* *Scendere*
Go away	{ *Partir* *S'en aller*	{ *Andar via* *Partire* *Andarsene*

These are the simplest examples, and the student should keep the alternatives in mind. Apart from these, there are a surprising number of compound phrases with adverbs where Italian and English idiom coincide: *Dar via*, 'to give away'; *gettar via*, 'to throw away'; *è via*, 'he is away'; *tirar fuori*, 'to pull out'; *sembri un po' giù*, 'you look rather down'; *buttar (scriver) giù sulla carta*, 'to put (write) down on paper'; *metter su casa*, 'to set up house'.

§ **73.** *Magari.* This is a rather elusive adverb. The following uses are distinguishable.

(a) *Magari=perfino*, a strong 'even', especially used in passing from weaker to stronger statement.

> Amare può consistere...nel riprendere, nel correggere, nel rimproverare—**magari** nel frustare a sangue colle parole. (Papini.)

> Il popolino del suo quartiere...gli fornisce degli alleati che nelle osterie lo difendono vociando **e magari** lo aiutano con piccoli prestiti a campare alla meno peggio. (Angioletti.)

N.B. Italian usually says *E magari* where we should say '**or** even'.

(b) *Magari=anche*, 'even (if)' in conditionals lacking *se* [§ 37(a)].

> **Magari** fosse così non lo direi.
> Even if it were, I shouldn't say so.

(c) *Magari* is concessive (= 'though', etc. in a phrase without a verb).

> ...*accontentandosi che un' idea lo nutra e lo conforti **magari** per un giorno solo.* (Ojetti.)
> ...feed and comfort him, though (if) only for a day.

> '*Hai un tavolino e un mazzo di tarocchi?*'
> '***Magari** un po' unti, ma li ho.*' (Fogazzaro.)
> 'Have you a card-table and a pack?'
> 'Well, they may be a bit greasy, but I've got them.'

(d) *Magari* emphasizes the subjunctive of wish.

> ***Magari** lo facesse!*   'I wish to goodness he'd do it.'

From this comes the elliptic use of *magari* alone to express a wish, e.g.:

> *Quando la mamma minacciava di andarsene era questo stesso diavolo che suggeriva al giovane di gridare:*
> '***Magari**! Così saremo liberi della tua tirannia.*' (Deledda.)
> When his mother threatened to go away, the same devil inside him impelled the boy to shout:
> ...'I only wish you would! Then we shall be free....'

(e) *Magari* is sometimes a strong expression of agreement.

> '*Non la pensi così?*' '*Magari.*'
> 'Don't you agree?' 'I do indeed (I certainly do, etc.).'

§ 74. *Affatto.* This may mean:

(a) 'Altogether', either in affirmative or in negative phrases. *Affatto cieco*, 'quite blind'; *non affatto cieco*, 'not quite blind'.

> *Non ancora le molli fogge di Francia han trasformato **affatto** le sembianze della città sobria e pudica.* (Carducci.)
> Not yet have the effeminate fashions of France altogether changed the features....

(b) 'At all', in negative sentences. This usage is condemned by Rankin ('Idiomatic Italian Composition', p. 41), who has certainly good authorities behind him (e.g. Fornaciari). On the other hand it is given without comment by Petrocchi (*rinforza la negazione*), and it is used by many good writers including some Tuscans (Fucini, Papini). It is particularly common in the set phrase *niente affatto*, 'not at all'.

> *O non abbaiava **affatto**, o se abbaiava la voce era tanto fioca....* (Fucini.)
> Either the dog didn't bark at all, or if it did....

Since the double use of *non affatto* in fact exists, the translator of Italian must consider carefully in a given passage whether the sense is 'not altogether' or 'not at all'.[1]

§ 75. *Anzi.* This strengthens or corrects a previous statement, and varies in sense between 'indeed (in fact)', 'or rather', and 'on the contrary'.

> *Era magro, **anzi** allampanato.*
> He was thin, indeed (in fact) painfully thin.
>
> *Anche il contadino rise, si calmò **ed anzi** ('and indeed') fece portare da casa sua un bottiglione di vino.* (Deledda.)
>
> *Ascoltò, **anzi** mi lasciò parlare a lungo.*
> He listened, or rather he let me talk, for a long time.
>
> *Non disamava le liti, **anzi** ci gongolava.*
> He didn't dislike quarrels; on the contrary, he revelled in them.
>
> *Il freddo diventa più acuto. Il Battello* (pedlar) *non se ne accorge. **Anzi** ha caldo, **anzi** è sudato.* (Fucini.)

Two notes on word-order:

(a) *Anzi* meaning 'indeed' is sometimes postponed, e.g.:

> *È curioso come la voce ingrandisca nei cimiteri, così grande **anzi** diventa che si finisce col tacere.* (Panzini.)
> It's strange how loud one's voice sounds in a churchyard, so loud indeed that....

---

[1] There is similar ambiguity in Greek over οὐ πάνυ.

(b) *Anzi* meaning 'on the contrary' is sometimes put as the last word of one sentence instead of the first word of the next. E.g. _the example already given might be repunctuated:

> *Non disamava le liti, anzi. Ci gongolava.*

§ 76. *Sì, no.*

(a) In familiar style (spoken or written) *no* may be used at the end of a phrase instead of *non* earlier, e.g.:

> *Questo si fa da loro, da noi **no** (= ma **non** da noi).*
> *Il discorso **no** ma l' accento di Lelia fu impertinente.* (Fogazzaro.)

Se no is of course always said for 'if not' when there is no verb.[1] Sometimes, not often, *Se sì* is said for 'if so'.

(b) *Sì* and *no* may replace a repeated verb.

> *Loro vanno al teatro? — Lui sì, io no.*
> 'Are you going to the theatre?' 'He is, but I'm not.'

(c) *Sì* emphasizes one of a pair of contrasted phrases.

> *Un sughero che resta **sì** a galla, ma è in balia dell' onde.* (Ojetti.)
> A cork which certainly keeps afloat (OR which does keep afloat) but is at the mercy of the waves.

> *Non è ricco, ma è spendereccio **sì**.*
> He isn't rich but he is extravagant.

In such phrases as this ('not X but Y'), *non* is often strengthened by *già* (= 'indeed'), and *ma...sì* is often replaced by *bensì* or *sibben(e)*,[2] e.g.:

> *Non è **già** ricco, **bensì** (**sibbene**) è spendereccio.*

> *Dopo il ravvedimento, egli appare **sì** un uomo nuovo, ma non **già** così nuovo come sembra a primo aspetto.* (Graf.)

---

[1] The use of *Se meno* in the same sense is disapproved by the stricter grammarians.

[2] Sharply to be distinguished from *sebbene*, 'though'.

*Li vede chiarissimamente, ma non come li vedevo io, scaltri e adulatori, **bensì** abbagliati dal suo genio e pentiti di non avervi per tanti anni creduto.* (Angioletti.)

(d) *Sì che* gives emphasis with implied contrast. E.g. having rejected a number of things in a shop, one finally says *Questo sì che mi piace*, 'Ah! I do like this one'. [The *che* here is a vague 'that', and the phrase represents roughly: 'This thing, it is true that it pleases me.' *Sì che* so used has no connection with consecutive *sì che* (*sicchè*), 'so that'.]

(e) *E sì che* = 'and yet'.

*Anche Jacopo la chiamava Marilù...; **e sì ch'** ella avrebbe mille e mille volte preferito esser chiamata mamma.* (Negri.)

*Cominciò a non poter più dormire. **E sì che** andava a letto stanco morto.* (Negri.)

*Io lo sentivo il senso di ripugnanza, **e sì che** facevo di tutto per vincermi.* (Cicognani.)

(f) *Sì e no* not only means 'about', with numerals (e.g. *venti libri sì e no*, 'some twenty books')—but also 'imperfectly', 'vaguely', 'dimly', 'half-', in which senses it is much used in descriptive passages.

*Si sentivano **sì e no** ('faintly') nell' aria inquieta e buia gli aliti delle rose...Si vedevan **sì e no** ('dimly') le frondi spargersi in qua e in là.* (Fogazzaro.)

*Della borgata s' intravvedeva **sì e no** ('vaguely') la parte estrema.* (Borgese.)

*...quel lieto vecchio, coperto **sì e no** ('half-covered') da un mantelluccio ragnato e rappezzato.* (Papini.)

Somewhat different are the following:

*Fra il **sì** e il **no** della luce.* (Negri.)

In the half-light.

*Una barchetta che **or sì** or **no** spuntava dietro l'orlo di acciaio delle onde.* (Angioletti.)

A little boat appearing and disappearing behind the steely rim of the waves.

§ 77. *Tanto* is often used like *tant' è* ('anyhow', 'in any case').

> *Non adirarti, **tanto** oramai la tua collera è inutile.* (Deledda.)
> Don't lose your temper—**anyhow** it's no good getting angry now.

This is surely the meaning of *tanto* in the proverb: *Come disse colui che cadde da cavallo, **tanto** volevo scendere*—'I wanted to get off anyhow'. (Hoare, under *tanto* 9, translates 'I did so want to get off'.)

COMBINED ADVERBS OF PLACE

§ 78. In such phrases as 'near here', 'in there', Italian uses two adverbs in the reverse of English order.[1]

> *Qui sotto*, under here.
> *Là dentro*, in there.
> *Qua fuori*, out here.
> *Qui oltre*, round about here.
> *Là presso* (*vicino*), near there.
> *Lì accanto*, just by there.
> *Qui dirimpetto*, opposite here.
> *Là attorno*, all round there.

The Italian adverbs combine into one word in *laggiù, lassù, quaggiù, quassù*.

§ 79. Adverbs in *-oni*. There are a number of useful and idiomatic adverbs in *-oni* which are usually equivalent to an Italian gerund or an English participle.

With *stare*, etc.:

> (*a*) *cavalcioni*, astride, a-straddle.
> (*a*) *ciondoloni*, dangling.
> *coccoloni*, squatting.
> *penzoloni*, hanging.

---

[1] The two Italian words in each case seem obviously adverbs. I do not presume to determine what parts of speech the English words are.

With *andare*, etc.:

> (*a*) *balzelloni*, skipping.
> *barcolloni*, tottering, staggering.
> *carponi* or *carpon carponi*, crawling, on all fours.
> (*a*) *gironi*, roaming about.
> *gobboni*, stooping, hunched up.
> (*a*) *saltelloni*, hopping.
> (*a*) *tastoni*, (*a*) *tentoni*, groping.
> *trambelloni*, reeling.
> *zoppiconi*, limping.

With *stare* or *cadere*:

> (*a*) *bocconi*, flat on one's face.
> (*in*) *ginocchioni*, kneeling, on one's knees.

With *andare* or *cadere*:

> *capitomboloni*, head over heels.
> (*a*) *ruzzoloni*, rolling (e.g. downstairs).

V

CONJUNCTIONS

§ **80.** *Che.*

(a) *Che* sometimes = *allorchè.*

> *A Venezia s' arrivò* ***che*** *sorgeva il sole.*
> We got to V. when the sun was rising (OR, PERHAPS BETTER,
> When we got to V. the sun was rising).

(b) *Che* sometimes = *sicchè, di modo che.*

> *Il sole indora tutta la facciata,* ***che*** *non ne perdo un particolare.*
> (Ojetti.)
> The front is (so brightly) lit by the sun that I don't miss
> a single detail.

> '*Buona notte*' *disse,* ***che*** *quasi non la si udì.* (Negri.)
> 'Good night', she said, (so softly) that she could scarcely be
> heard.

> *Una folla* ***che*** *non si camminava.* (Pirandello.)
> (Such) a crowd that there was no room to walk.

This usage is specially common with expressions of pleasure and
admiration.

> *La processione procede...bene spaziata e cadenzata* ***che è un***
> ***piacere.*** (Ojetti.)
> ...so well in time that it's a pleasure to watch (OR MERELY
> delightfully in time).

> *La notte si passa* ***che è un piacere*** ('delightfully'), *fra pette-*
> *golezzi, notizie inedite, chiacchiere varie.* (Serra.)

Going further, one may say of an exquisitely-dressed woman:
Vestiva ***che era un paradiso.***

(c) *Che* is sometimes a weak 'for'[1]—so weak that English would leave it unexpressed.

> *Va su e sbrigati e torna giù che t' aspetto.* (Fogazzaro.)
>
> Go up and get it over and come down again; I'll wait for you.

§ 81. *Non che; se non che.* Without a verb, or with infinitive, *non che* sometimes means 'not only', sometimes 'not only not'. (These opposite possibilities go back to an original ellipse—'I do not say so-and-so' or 'not to speak of so-and-so'.)

(a) *Non che* = 'not only'.

> *Lo cacciò con busse **non che** con parolacce.*
>
> *Tendenze...corrompitrici, **nonchè** delle anime, dell' arte stessa.* (Graf.)

It is journalese to use *non che* merely for 'and' or 'also'.

(b) *Non che* = 'not only not' (most often with a preceding negative, but sometimes without).

> *Non voleva...più niente; **non che** la gratitudine di lui, ma neppure il ricordo.* (Pirandello.)
>
> *Nessuno poteva, **non che udirlo**, vederlo.* (Fogazzaro.)
>
> ***Non che** accorrere al richiamo, neppur si voltava.* (Pirandello.)
>
> *L' esperienza mistica e la liturgia, **non che** escludersi, si accordano e si integrano a vicenda.* (Manacorda.)

Non che in this latter use is often a good translation of 'far from'; others are *anzi che*, *invece che* (see § 82). *Lungi (lontano) dal far qualcosa* is possible Italian, but less common and less idiomatic.[2]

(c) *Se non che* = 'only' at the beginning of a phrase.

> Shakespeare is sad stuff, only one must not say so.
>
> *Roba dozzinale lo S., **se non che** mai non si deve dirlo.*

---

[1] The same word as a STRONG 'for' (= 'because, since') is usually given an accent (*chè*), but one cannot depend on this.

[2] E.g. *Donna Fedele, lontana dal sospettare il vero, credette....* (Fogazzaro.) *Gemme che il tempo, lungi dall' offuscare, ha dimostrato sempre più vive e lucenti.* (Manacorda.)

> ...*un vecchio falegname, il quale aveva nome mastr' Antonio,*
> *se non che tutti lo chiamavano maestro Ciliegia.* (Collodi.)

> *Il movimento della folla...ricorda,* **se non che** *in proporzioni*
> *minori, quella moltitudine....* (Fucini.)

§ 82. *Anzi che, più che, invece che* ('rather than'); *oltre che* ('besides').
All these resemble each other (a) in being used with infinitives or
without verbs; (b) in being usually placed first though their English
equivalents would be placed second. This is a highly important
point, for unless one is familiar with the order it is easy to reverse
the sense. One says in English: 'He wanted help rather than advice.'
One says in Italian (usually): 'He wanted, rather than advice, help.'
In translating from Italian, there is the choice of (1) keeping the
adverbial formula and changing the phrase order or (2) changing the
adverbial formula and keeping the phrase order, e.g.:

> *Voleva, più che consiglio, aiuto.*

(1) He wanted help rather than advice.

(2) He wanted advice **less** than help.

It was **not** advice he wanted **so much as** help.

We may now proceed to less simple examples.

> *Quando si vorrebbe anzi che camminare volare.*
> When one would rather fly than walk.

> ...*la pittura fiorentina e veneziana, dove la natura più che*
> *osservata è contemplata, più che copiata è scelta, e lo*
> *spettatore, più che percosso dalle dure parole e dalle rotte*
> *grida, è rapito dalla musica delle forme e dei colori.*
> (Ojetti.)
> ...where nature is rather contemplated than observed, rather
> selected than copied, and the beholder is **not** so much
> struck...as enraptured....

> *Pareva lo dicesse più che per rassicurarla, per un istinto di*
> *crudeltà.* (Deledda.)
> He seemed to speak thus **less** through a wish to cheer her
> than through an instinct for hurting her.

*Il riordinamento in quelle sezioni di retroguardia più che per gli
    ordini che arrivavano dai comandi s' era operato per
    iniziative sparse di gruppi.* (Bontempelli.)

The rearrangement of these sections was due more to group
    initiative than to official orders.

*Ecco perchè la Pisana rassomiglia, più che a Carmen del
    Mérimée e a qualcuna delle donne della Sand e del Balzac,
    alla Natalia del Tolstoi.* (Albertazzi.)

For this reason Nievo's Pisana is less like Carmen, etc. than
    she is like Tolstoi's Natalie.

Invece che dall' ombra il refrigerio viene dai prati acquosi.
    (Ojetti.)

The coolness comes from the meadows instead of from the
    shade (OR 'not from the shade but from the meadows').

Perchè noi, oltre che adorarlo, impariamo ad amarlo. (Albertini.)
That we may learn to love him as well as worship him (OR
    'not only to worship him but to love him too').

§ **83.** Omission of *che*. The omission of *che* is more frequent than
the grammars suggest. Grandgent, for instance (op. cit. p. 69, n. 1),
is far too timid on the subject.

The following distinctions are to be made:

(a) Relative *che* should never be omitted. If any exception may
possibly be allowed, it is the rare but well-established usage of
dropping relative *che* after *di quello* in comparative sentences, e.g.:

*Nè Raffaello avrebbe dipinto la trasfigurazione ideale dell' umano
    meglio **di quello facesse** il Petrarca nel personaggio di
    Laura.* (Carducci.)

*Un libro il quale... non è men vivo oggi **di quello fosse** mezzo
    secolo fa.* (Graf.)

But here also the student would be well advised to write in full *meglio
di quello che facesse* [or else, of course, *meglio che (non) facesse*].[1]

---

[1] In much old Italian, relatives are dropped freely enough (cf. Compagni
especially). D' Azeglio imitates the construction in his Wardour Street historical
novels, e.g. *Non v' erano altri discorsi che delle feste si dovevano fare.*

(b) *Che* as conjunction with subjunctive clauses may and should sometimes be omitted.

    (i) With impersonal *pare*, *che* is omitted more often than not. *Pare sia vero; pare siano partiti.*

    (ii) After verbs of hoping, wishing, thinking, saying, knowing, *che* is omitted less often than in (i), but still fairly often. Omission may be desirable if another *che* (relative or conjunction) occurs at close quarters.

    Speriamo non ti venga in mente di andarci. (Deledda.)

    Non voleva uscisse la notizia. (Bontempelli.)

    Credendo fosse venuta. (Fogazzaro.)

    Mobilia che mi dissero fosse antica.

    Desidero lo sappiano tutti. (Bontempelli.)

    Le accuse che supponeva gli fossero state fatte. (Fogazzaro.)

    (iii) *Che* is fairly often omitted with clauses of fearing; the optional *non* is then usually put in, especially if the periphrastic subjunctive (§ 39) is used.

    Temevo (non) fosse venuto.

    ...*avvicinarsi ad esso col tremore e col rispetto con cui s' aprono le vecchie tombe, non abbiano i corpi ad apparire* ('lest the bodies should appear') *intatti per un istante e subito cadere in polvere.* (Ojetti.)

    (iv) *Che* may also be omitted: from the compounds *a meno che* and *per poco che*; after *inutile*, *difficile*, *facile*; after one or two verbs hard to classify. The following examples are typical. The general point of omission is that the result should look neat rather than careless; again, the presence nearby of another *che* may be a reason for omission.

    A meno non si scuopra che....(Cecchi.)

    Per poco il discorso accennasse a parare per quel verso ('if the conversation showed the slightest sign of taking that turn').... (Bacchelli.)

    Se vuol raggiungere il Tempo, inutile lei si metta a corrergli dietro. (Cecchi.)

Non è facile noi si venga mai a un ponderato esame di quanto gli dobbiamo. (Ojetti.)

Il contadino gli prese tutte e due le mani, e ci mancò poco non gliele baciasse. (Tozzi.)

Il vecchio giardiniere che non amava si mancasse così di riguardo ai suoi fiori. (Deledda.)

Sapevo che bastava guardassi un po' meglio. (Cecchi.)

(c) *Che* as a conjunction with indicative is also sometimes omitted. It may freely be dropped from the compounds *appena che* and *secondo che*, but beyond this it is better not to go. Some good writers omit *che* after *ogni volta* with indicative [e.g. *Ogni volta si vedeva nello specchio* (Bacchelli)] and some journalists omit it after *ora* [e.g. *ora ci siamo,* 'now (that) we are here']. These uses seem undesirable, especially when the result is ambiguity (if only for the moment). In the uses collected under (b), the subjunctive is a warning of the subordinate construction; here there is none.

§ **84.** Use of *E* with other meanings than 'and'.

(a) *E* may mean 'then, very well', in which sense it usually (i) follows an 'if' clause or (ii) precedes an imperative; it may do both, and it tends to draw a personal pronoun with it.

(i) *Che se*[1] *per niuna tale strada si entra in Firenze, ed io in Firenze non rientrerò mai* ('If..., **then** I will never...'). (Carducci.)

(ii) *Vuoi comprare il podere di Reggio; e tu compralo.* (Tozzi.) You want to buy the farm; very well, buy it.

'Se parli così me ne vado'. 'E tu vattene'. (Albertini.)

(i) and (ii) together. *E se poi Garibaldi vuole la repubblica, e che la repubblica gliela diano!* (Bacchelli.)

Se lei dice davvero, e allora mi dia quello che vuole. (Fucini.)

---

[1] It. *che se* = Fr. *que si* = Lat. *quodsi* = 'and if' or 'but if'.

5-2

One example with neither (i) nor (ii):

> *Lei mi contesta il credito? E* ('Very well then') *io verrò a mangiare da lei.* (Cicognani.)

(b) *E* may also mean 'What of...?', 'What about...?' *E tuo padre?* 'What about your father?' This use of *e* is so distinct from the connective use that *ma* may precede it immediately ('But what of', etc.).

> *Ma e Mario?* (Bontempelli.)

> *Ma e il mezzo per andare a Comacchio?* (Panzini.)

> *Ma, e se venisse a Roma subito?*[1] (Fogazzaro.)

(c) In some contexts, Italian says *Ed è, E sono, Ed era*, where we say 'This is', 'These are', 'This was', or 'Namely'.

> *Mettiamo in sodo un primo fatto importante, ed è che...* ('namely that...'). (Graf.)

> *Due soggetti non lasciano dubbio sull' interpretazione e sono* ('namely' or 'I mean') *il fregio della Centauromachia e quello dell' Amazonomachia.* (Della Seta.)

> *Erano ormai sostenuti da una virtù grande, ma più propria a penitenti e magari a martiri che non a dei soldati; ed era la rassegnazione.* (Bacchelli.)

§ 85. *Se.*

(a) *Se* is used to repeat a question just asked by someone else.

> '*O il sor Federigo come verrebbe a essere di lei?*'
> '*Zio. O che lo conosci?*'
> '*Se lo conosco! Siamo stati ragazzi insieme.*' (Fucini.)
> 'What relation is Federigo to you?'
> 'My uncle. Why, do you know him?'
> 'Do I know him? We were boys together.'

> '*Che è grosso dimolto questo Pesce-cane?*' *domandò Pinocchio....*
> '*Se gli è grosso!*' *replicò il Delfino.* (Collodi.)

---

[1] This is quite distinct from the somewhat academic usage (found, e.g. in Carducci's prose) by which *non pure...ma e* means 'not only...but also'.

(b) *Ma se* sometimes introduces a protest against a doubt or mistake on the part of the last speaker.

'*Ne sei proprio sicuro?*'
'*Ma se ti dico di esservi stato io stesso!*'
'Are you quite sure?'
'Look here, I tell you I was there myself.'

'*Pareva un simbolo, quel povero cavallo.*'
'*Ma se era un mulo, mamma!*' (Deledda.)
'The poor horse looked quite a symbolic creature.'
'But, mother, it was a mule!'

PREPOSITIONS

§ 86. Prepositions omitted or repeated.

Italian is not so strict as French in repeating prepositions before every noun they govern. The following are typical examples of omission:

> *Il gruppo delle educande coi vestiti bianchi di mussola, i grembiuli neri, e le cinture di varii colori...prese un aspetto gaio* (= *coi grembiuli, colle cinture*). (Serao.)
>
> *Un paesaggio fioccoso di tetti, muri e ringhiere* (= *di muri e di ringhiere*). (Bontempelli.)

Nevertheless, Italian repeats prepositions where English would not (cf. Ojetti's long sentence in § 82), and the student should simply avoid extremes.

§ 87. *Con* = English 'to' with nouns of emotion ('astonishment', 'disappointment', etc.).

> *Con molto dispiacere de' suoi scolaretti ma con piacere grandissimo del direttore.* (Pirandello.)
>
> To the great regret...to the extreme delight....

§ 88. *In breve* and *fra breve* both mean 'soon, in a short time', but *in breve* is used of the past, *fra breve* of the future: *Tornò in breve, tornerà fra breve.* (*Dopo poco* = *in breve; fra poco* = *fra breve.*)

§ 89. Preposition and article. In some set phrases, the article is dropped with one preposition but used with another: *In presenza di* but *alla presenza di; di solito* but *al solito* and *per il solito; d' improvviso* but *all' improvviso; di subito* but *in un subito.*

WORD-ORDER

§ 90. Italian has what we may call a normal word-order which is very much like our own: roughly—subject, verb, object or predicate, with adverbial phrases at beginning or end of the sentence. There is no need to illustrate this, or to remark on the few exceptions (e.g. position of pronouns and adjectives) which all grammars discuss. [For additional notes on normal usage see §§ 2(d), 23(c), 31(c), 32(b), 57–8, 75, 82.]

§ 91. But Italian departs from this normal usage much more readily than English (at least than modern English). In some cases there is an alternative word-order which makes little or no difference of emphasis. In others there is a marked inversion where emphasis is important.

§ 92. Alternative word-order with little or no emphasis.

(a) When there is no object-noun, a subject-noun may follow the verb. This is very common indeed.

> *Scese la notte.... Lo diceva lo zio.... Era inutile ormai ogni soccorso.*

(b) Even when an object-noun is there, the subject-noun is sometimes inverted, so that the two come together.

(i) Subject first.

> *Cercava il padre di Palmirina rifugio, quiete e perdono.* (Pea.)

> *Su questa basi edificò Manzoni la sua tragedia storica.* (De Sanctis.)

(ii) Object first.

> *In un canto aspettava l' ultima pennellata un acquerello.* (Verga.)

> *Al di sopra...rizzava il capo il campanile.* (Verga.)

But this is not a common usage, and many writers avoid it.

(c) Adverbs, and sometimes longer phrases, may come between *con* and the noun it governs.

> *Una scatola con dentro dei cioccolatini.*
> A box with chocolates in.

> *Una busta con su scritta qualche parola.*
> An envelope with a few words written on it.

> *Con di sopra un cielo limpido.*
> With a clear sky above.

Further examples:

> *Con fra le mani, come il famoso Medici di Sandro, una medaglia del Pisanello.* (Soffici.)

> *Con appena, a indicare la presenza dell' uomo, qualche bianca borgata sonnolenta.* (Praz.)

> *Con in più, soggiunse Evandro, la presenza....* (Bontempelli.)

(d) *Da* with a pronoun often comes between a noun and a passive participle (a construction which may conveniently replace a relative clause).[1]

> *Le parole da lui adoperate.*
> The words used by him (the words he used).

(e) The objects or adverbs *poco, molto, tanto, tutto, niente, nulla, altro, qualcosa* often precede the verb.

> *Poco ci rimise e molto ne ricavò.*
> He lost little by it and gained a good deal.

> *Tutto osavano e niente temevano.*
> They dared everything and feared nothing.

---

[1] *Da* with a noun was once used in the same position, and survivals of this may still be found but should scarcely be imitated, e.g. *tutti gli alti valori dalla novissima barbarie tenuti a vile.* (D' Annunzio.)

Further examples:

> *Quella bellezza dignitosa che niente ha di giovanile e tanto*
> *d' immortale.* (Fogazzaro.)

> *Un fiorentino vero a tutto può rinunziare e tutto può sopportare.*
> (Papini.)

> *Chi tutto questo non sente e non intende, è fuori del cristianesimo.*
> (Manacorda.)

> *La scienza di ieri in tanto vale in quanto ha creato la scienza*
> *d' oggi.* (Ojetti.)

> *Qualcosa di vero seppe vedere.* (Papini.)

> *Però tu qualche cosa sai.* (Fogazzaro.)

> *Ma Dante ad altro ricorre.* (Papini.)

> *Di quest' affascinante bandito ben poco appresi fino a circa*
> *pagina duecento, e molto appresi invece di usi e costumi*
> *delle più iperboree isole scozzesi.* (Praz, on reading Scott's
> 'Pirate'.)

(f) In some sentences where English has a superlative plural or collective plural ('the most beautiful things', 'all the beautiful things') followed by a relative, the best Italian translation is *ciò che*, *quel che* or *quanto* with a possessive singular. Two points of word-order are then to be noted. (i) In any case, the possessive comes *inside* the relative clause. (ii) If the relative clause is short, the possessive follows the verb; if it is long enough and the rhythm appropriate, the possessive may precede the verb.

(i) He gave them the most beautiful things he had.
Donò loro quanto aveva di più bello.

All the beautiful things he had.
Tutto ciò che aveva di bello.

(ii) All the good things he hoped for and the bad things he feared.
Tutto quel che di bello sperava e di brutto temeva.

Sometimes an Italian relative clause may replace an English noun.
The poet's loftiest **fancies**.
Ciò che di più alto aveva immaginato il poeta.

73

(g) *Poi* is often placed between *per* and an infinitive.

> *Ebbe la tentazione di...far capovolgere la barca per poi, naturalmente, salvare i naufraghi.* (Angioletti.)

§ 93. Inversion for emphasis.

(a) It is sometimes desirable in English to suspend the subject for the sake of a special effect. In some cases it is enough to place 'there' before the verb: 'There came a time...', 'There seemed to him to be...', 'If there passed my window one tithe of those...' ('Zuleika Dobson'). Italian easily gives the same order without inserting anything: *Venne un tempo..., Gli sembrò..., Se venisse a passare....* In obituary notices, our more solemn journals provide an artificial subject in order to postpone the logical subject: 'The death occurred yesterday in his London residence of Mr So-and-So.' The Italian equivalent is: *È morto*[1] *ieri nella sua casa londinese il signor tal de' tali.*

(b) Exceptionally, English inverts nouns and adjectives for emphasis: 'Talent, Mr Micawber has; capital, Mr Micawber has not.' 'This hero, if hero he may be called.' 'Amorous I may be, bigamous no' (Gordon Harker). All such phrases can go into Italian as they stand.

(c) The following instances show idiomatic inversion of a kind too bold for English. (I omit the well-known formulas of noun—resumptive pronoun—verb, e.g. *Questo cappello se lo comprò a Parigi,* and of the postponed emphatic pronoun, e.g. *Stavolta avrà da lavorare lui.*) Notice that English and Italian sometimes get the same general effect by stressing different words; e.g. in the first example below, Italian stresses the adjective (by position); English stresses the verb (by pronunciation or italics).

> *Mìa moglie sarà...sarà come tu vuoi; ma intelligente è.* (Pirandello.)
>
> My wife may be—whatever you like to call her; but she **is** clever.

---

[1] Or with greater gentility, *Si è spento.*

74

Se la lingua non conoscerai bene.... (De Amicis.)

If you don't know the **language** properly.

Mi trattava di delinquente.... Gli dissi che un delinquente non ero. (Bacchelli.)

He spoke as if I were a criminal.... I told him I was **not** a criminal.

'Sarà quel che sarà. E sta' tranquillo che non verrò da te per l' elemosina.' 'Da me e da altri che me verrai, con tutto codesto orgoglio fradicio.' (Borgese.)

'What must be, must be. And you needn't be afraid that I shall come begging to you.' 'You **will** come to me, and to others as well, for all your filthy pride.'

Pareva...che una musica, non potuta udire[1] dalle altre, ella udisse. (Serao.)

It was as if **she** heard music the others could not.

'Ammazzeremo anche lui', disse quietamente. 'Come — dissi — Herzen ammazzeresti?' (Bacchelli.)

'We'll kill him too', he said calmly.—'What!' I said. 'You'd kill **Herzen**?'

Further examples:

E un' altra strana sensazione provai.... (Cecchi.)

No, no. Non era buono come pareva.... Cattivo era. (Pirandello.)

Mai nomina se stesso, ma di continuo a se allude. (Papini.)

Forzare non vorrei ma tentare bisogna. (Fogazzaro.)

'Oh che stai facendo, con tanta cura?' 'Ingrato d' uno zio...di te mi occupo.' (Leo di Castelnovo.)

Le nebbie s' erano diradate, ma proprio sereno non fu mai. (Tozzi.)

Tullia non era bella. Belli erano soli gli occhi. (Bontempelli.)

Se questa fortuna non avrai.... (De Amicis.)

---

[1] On the construction of *non potuta udire*, see § 33.

75

È arrivato l' ambasciatore! Anche l' ambasciatore mi mandano.
  (Borgese.)

Lei dunque un uomo pacifico è. (Pirandello.)

*Non bastano quei pochi malanni che ho; anche sordo ho da
  essere.* (Fogazzaro.)

Persuaditi che con te o senza di te io regina voglio essere.
  (Albertini.)

*Gli scrittori, nelle luminose distanze del tempo, non uomini
  sembreranno, ma semidei.* (Cecchi.)

Ma non rise. Ridere Eliseo non la vide mai in tutto quel tempo.
  (Borgese.)

*Mi par impossibile di aver a restare sopra un campo di battaglia
  ma impossibile non è.* (Fogazzaro.)

'*Ho avuto torto a stimarlo troppo male.*' '*Torto? Ragione
  avevate, ragionissima.*' (Bacchelli.)

*La vendetta del popolo di Napoli, che accolse con festa ogni re,
  e ogni re abbandonò al suo destino.* (Panzini.)

VIII

NOTES ON CERTAIN ITALIAN WORDS

§ 94. (Since the following notes are by way of supplementing and also correcting the standard 'Italian Dictionary' of Hoare, I must in decency preface them with the quite sincere statement that I think his work in many ways admirable and his general knowledge of Italian of a standard which I have not the slightest pretention to reach. But the making of a really satisfactory dictionary is beyond the unaided powers of any individual; he must be able to use the research and criticism of many scholars working from many different points of view on both of the languages concerned. In the case of Italian and English a great deal of the work necessary has yet to be done, and what follows is a small contribution only to what should be in the future an important part of Anglo-Italian studies.

Hoare's main weaknesses are two. In the matter of ecclesiastical terms (liturgical, philosophical, theological) he is as untrustworthy as the run of his fellow-lexicographers in this country.[1] Corrections here would be beyond my present purpose. But he is also far too free in assigning equivalent meanings to Italian and English words of the same derivation when these words have in fact developed differently in the two languages. Most of my observations bear on distinctions here. I add one or two words which he has omitted altogether.)

Accusare (*un malore*). H. 'to **admit** not feeling quite well'. Rather 'to **complain of** feeling ill'. So the doctor in a story of Annie Vivanti's asks his patient *Quali disturbi accusa?* 'What symptoms do you complain of?' Cf. Deledda: *Si mise a letto, accusando un falso principio di febbre. Accusare* has also, like

[1] His rendering of *iperdulia*, for instance, deserves to stand with Fowler's definition of Thomism.

French *accuser*, the sense of 'show, reveal, betray', e.g. *Senza poter pronunziar parola che accusasse il suo profondo turbamento.* (Fucini.)

Alterare. H. 'to alter'. Usually 'to change for the worse'. *Ha alterato la verità,* 'He has corrupted (misrepresented) the truth'; *Questo altera la salute,* 'This is bad for (impairs) one's health'.

Amorevole. H. 'affectionate'. Yes, but the word is sometimes weaker; e.g. *parole amorevoli* may mean hardly more than 'friendly (OR kindly) words'.

Argomento. Add the common sense 'theme, subject', e.g. *un argomento doloroso.*

Associazione. H. 'as English'. Not in the sense of PERSONAL association(s), for which in different contexts one will require e.g. *il frequentare (praticare, bazzicare), le relazioni, i rapporti, la domestichezza, la convivenza, l' intrinsechezza, il legame (i legami), l' ambiente sociale.*

Autista = chauffeur, car-driver. Not in H.

Banda. Add under H. 7 (= *parte*) the meaning 'time', e.g. *da trent' anni a questa banda,* 'for the last thirty years'.

Batteria. Add: *Scoprire le batterie,* 'to give the show away'.

Bellezza. Add: *Che bellezza!,* 'How lovely, how splendid!'. *La bellezza di* with a figure is used of a high price, high speed, etc. *M' ha costato la bellezza di mille lire; Correvano alla bellezza di settanta chilometri.*

Bene (the noun) sometimes means 'love'. In old verse it is often used for the loved person, as *Caro mio ben!* In modern prose it may have the abstract sense of 'affection'. This is combined with the commoner sense in Albertazzi's sentence: *Lei m' ha fatto comprendere che bene* (blessing) *sarebbe stato alla mia vita il bene* (love) *di una sorella.* Note also the phrase *tanto ben di Dio,* used like *tanta grazia di Dio,* for a profusion of something, especially food or wine.

Benpensanti (i) H. 'careful thinkers'. No: 'the orthodox'.

Bestia. H. 'beast'. Yes, but the common Italian use is the widest English one. Cows are *bestie* to any Italian, whereas in England it is chiefly the farmer who calls them 'beasts', and most townsfolk associate the word with fierce and exotic animals. *Bestia* used of persons indicates stupidity rather than 'beastliness'. *Che bestia sono stato!* 'What an idiot I've been!' On the other hand, *andare in bestia* (*diventare una bestia, imbestialire*) means 'to get into a rage'.

Brodo. Add: *Tutto fa brodo*, 'Everything comes in handy', 'It's all grist to one's mill'.

Caramella. Add the meaning 'monocle', with the derivative *caramellato*, 'monocled'.

Carnale. H. 'carnal'. The Italian has a less limited sense. *Un istinto carnale*, 'a feeling in the blood'. *Le qualità che lo fanno universale son legate a contingenze carnali* (Papini), 'are linked with physical contingencies'.

Coincidenza. H. 'as E.' Yes. But note (a) that the commonest Italian for 'coincidence' is *combinazione* ('*Che combinazione!*', '*Fu proprio una combinazione*') and (b) that *coincidenza* is used of a 'connection' in railway travelling.

Competente, competenza. H. 'as E.' Only in the limited senses of 'the competent authority', 'within the competence of the court', etc. In the general sense of 'capable', Italians say *bravo, capace, valente*, etc. 'She's a competent housewife', *È una brava massaia*. 'The task was beyond their competence', *Non erano da tanto*.

Compunto. H. 'remorseful, grieved'. Often has the sense of 'demure', e.g. of the conventional choirboy. Cf. Allodoli, *Bambini...tutti vestiti bene con un' aria compunta di gioia*.

Concludere. H. 'to conclude'. Often 'to effect', 'to carry things out'. *Discorre molto ma non conclude niente*, 'He talks a lot but never gets anything done'. Mr Belloc's 'Ineffectual Don' would be *Professore inconcludente*.

Consolare. H. 'to console'. Yes, but the reflexive *consolarsi* is often used of pleasure without any notion of consolation. *Me ne consolo tanto*, like *Me ne rallegro tanto*, 'I am very glad to hear it'.

Conveniente. H. 'convenient, suitable'. 'Convenient' in the archaic sense of 'seemly'. In the modern sense, 'convenient' is *comodo, opportuno*.

79

Copricapo (*il*). Like French *couvre-chef*, 'headgear, hat' (humorous or contemptuous). Not in H.; used by Fogazzaro.

Coraggio. H. 'courage'. Often pejorative, 'impertinence'.

Crema. May mean 'custard' also (the commonest use).

Differenza. Add: *a differenza di*, 'unlike'. *A differenza di suo fratello, si alza sempre presto.*

Disinvolto. H. 'self-possessed, cool'. Or merely 'easy' (in manner).

Disposizione. H. (1) 'disposition'. Not in the sense of 'temperament', which is *indole*, though the plural *disposizioni* sometimes approaches this sense.

Distratto. H. 'distracted'. No; 'absent-minded'.

Droga. H. 'drug'. Yes, in the wide but now obsolete sense in which various imported groceries might once be called 'drugs' (see 'O.E.D.' for examples). In the modern sense, 'drugs' in a general way are covered by *le medicine, i medicinali, i farmaci, i calmanti, i sonniferi;* but when their harmfulness is to be stressed one now says *gli stupefacenti.* A *drogheria* (H. 'grocer's or chemist's shop') is a place for selling *droghe*; hence never a chemist's shop (*farmacia*), and rather a special kind of grocer's —one where spices, salt, coffee, liqueurs are sold.

Enfasi, enfatico. H. 'as E.' Rather 'as French'. Noun and adjective are most often used of over-emphasis, rhetorical exaggeration, high-flown language, pomposity. 'He spoke with emphasis of the danger' might be *Sottolineò il pericolo* or *Ne parlò molto sul serio* or *Ne parlò, calcando le parole.*

Esperto. H. 'expert'. Rather 'experienced'. 'Expert'=*perito.*

Espresso. Add: as adjective or noun, *un* (*caffè*) *espresso*, 'a freshly made cup of coffee' (served in a café).

Evidenza. H. 'as E.' Not in the legal sense, which is *testimonianza, prova.*

Favoreggiare, favoreggiamento. H. 'to show partiality to'. Verb and noun are often pejorative, e.g. *favoreggiare una congiura*, 'to be involved in a plot'. Cf. Bacchelli: *A scagionar suo padre dal sospetto di favoreggiamento* ('complicity').

Formale. H. 'as E.' Not altogether. 'A formal invitation'=*un invito ufficiale.* *Una promessa formale*='a solemn promise'.

Formare, formarsi, formazione. H. 'as E.' Often used of moral or intellectual TRAINING.

Futile. H. 'as E.' May have a much weaker sense than 'futile', e.g. *questioni futili,* 'trifling matters'.

Gamba. Add: *In gamba,* 'brisk' (=*arzillo*); *essere in gamba,* 'to be hale and hearty'.

Gilda, guilda (la)='guild'. Not in H. Spelt *gilda* by Carducci and Bacchelli, *guilda* by Cecchi.

Grazioso. H. 'gracious'. This is a rather rare sense; the common one is 'pretty' or 'graceful'.

Illusione. H. 'as E.' No, not quite. It is often used of feelings and thoughts which are in fact illusory, but with emphasis on their pleasantness rather than their mistakenness. 'Dream' or 'fond hope' would sometimes be a good rendering.

Impressione. H. 'as E.' Usually; but in modern Italian is sometimes used by itself in the sense of *cattiva impressione. Fa impressione!* 'How shocking!' or 'How disagreeable!' There is a similar use of *Fa senso!*

Inconsistente, inconsistenza. H. 'as E.' Most used of something unreal or lacking solidity—an ill-grounded argument, a superficial mind, a character without depth, an 'insubstantial pageant'.

Indifferente. H. 'as E.' Not in the sense of 'poor, slight', which according to context is *mediocre, meschino, magro, da poco, di poco conto, di scarso valore.*

Infittire. H. 'to become thick'. Add: 'to become heavy, heavier' (of rain). *La pioggia infittiva.*

Inteso. Non darsene per inteso. H. '(a) to conceal one's knowledge of it, (b) to disregard advice or instructions'. Rather 'to take no notice' of something (whether one is aware of it or not). *La strada era diventata tutta un pantano e ci si andava fino a mezza gamba. Ma il burattino non se ne dava per inteso.* (Collodi.)

Inutile. H. 'useless'. So most often, but sometimes = 'unnecessary'; as in French. Cf. Fucini (in '*L' oriolo col cuculo*'): *La misura era presso a poco inutile* ('hardly necessary', 'scarcely called for'). And Praz: *È inutile che io mi soffermi su un altro passo romantico*, 'I need not pause over another romantic passage (in Dryden)'.

Macchina. Add the sense: 'motor-car'.

Maggioranza. H. 'majority'. Strictly speaking, should only be used of a nation or community with regard to its votes, desires, etc. Otherwise one says *la maggior parte*, *i più*, etc. 'In the majority of cases', *il più delle volte*.

Mestatore. Often used of a social or political agitator.

Morale (noun). Distinguish genders. *Il morale* = the MORAL(E) of an army, etc. *La morale* = morality, morals, or the moral of a story.

Occasione. H. 'as E.' The sense 'opportunity' is common in Italian. *L' occasione fa l' uomo ladro*.

Occorrere. Note that in the impersonal use the affirmative *occorre* practically coincides with *bisogna* ('one must'); but that while *non bisogna* means 'one must not', *non occorre* means 'one need not', 'there is no occasion'.

Ogni with a superlative means 'even the...': *da stancare ogni lettor più longanime* (Graf), 'enough to tire even the most long-suffering of readers'.

Onesto. H. 'honest in the widest sense'. Often 'decent', 'respectable', 'edifying'. In 'Our Mutual Friend', the garments and appurtenances of Bradley Headstone are all *onesti*. So one may say: *Appena si poteva onestamente partire*, 'As soon as we could **decently** get away'. Bacchelli calls a provincial shooting party *gli onesti protetti di Sant' Umberto* ('the **worthy** devotees of St Hubert'), and Bontempelli has: *All' onesto quadro* ('the **edifying** picture') *non manca neppure la figura del gatto domestico*.

Passione. Add the senses: (a) 'sorrow'; (b) 'keen desire, anxiety'. (a) *Aveva il cuore grosso dalla passione nel vedere il suo povero*

Pinocchio in quello stato compassionevale. (b) *Tormentato dalla passione di rivedere il suo babbo....* (Collodi.)

Petulante, petulanza. H. 'as E.' No; 'overbearing, arrogant'. 'Petulant' has the main idea of *scontroso* or *bizzoso* with an added suggestion of *smorfioso*.

Pianta sometimes means not 'plant' but 'tree'—chiefly in verse (cf. Leopardi, '*L' infinito*') but also in prose. In the '*Promessi Sposi*', c. 17, Renzo wonders whether to climb a tree, *arrampicarsi sur una pianta e star lì a aspettar l' aurora*; and the Fox and Cat hang up Pinocchio *al ramo di una grossa pianta detta la Quercia grande*. Cf. Albertini: *Abbracciato a una pianta, appoggiava l' orecchio al tronco*.

Portafoglio. H. 'portfolio'. Only in the political sense; in common use it means 'pocket-book', 'note-case'. 'Portfolio' is *cartella*.

Premere. H. 'to press'. Add the sense: 'to concern, interest, matter to one'. *Gli preme l' onore*, 'he holds his honour dear'. Cf. Bacchelli: *Non erano questi i motivi che premevano* ('mattered') *a lui*. Often impersonally. *Mi preme* ('I am anxious') *di mettere a posto le cose; gli premeva di tornare in patria.*

Principale (noun). Add the sense: 'senior partner' in business.

Puntino. Add: *cotto a puntino*, 'cooked to a turn'.

Questionare = 'to argue, dispute'. **Questionarsi** = 'to wrangle'.

Raccomandarsi. The commonest sense of the reflexive is 'to implore, entreat'. *Mi raccomando*, whether as a strong 'Please' or as 'Allow me' (H. 4), is merely a particular application of this. *Disse raccomandandosi*, 'he said imploringly'.

Resistente, resistere. H. 'as E.' The adjective is used of things that are STRONG or TOUGH (e.g. tools, bolts and bars, dress-materials). The verb is used not only of active resistance but of passive endurance. Carducci has the absolute use: *Il vecchio mondo resiste ancora* ('still holds out'). *Non resisto a qualche cosa* often means 'I can't stand it, can't put up with it'. This is a point that may easily be missed in translation. In Bonsanti's story, '*Fuga dell' Adriana*', the truant heroine tells her maid: *Di' al conte* *che non potevo resistere, ma tornerò.* The English reader might take this to mean 'I couldn't resist slipping away'. It actually means 'I couldn't face staying behind'.

Ridotto. Add *mal ridotto,* 'in a bad way', 'in a sorry plight'.

Risultare. H. 'as E.' Add the senses: (a) 'to become known', 'to emerge from the evidence' [used impersonally, as in § 37(i)]; (b) 'to prove' (with adjectives; cf. § 42).

Scandere. Add: *Scandere le sillabe* (*le parole*), 'to bring out every syllable, articulate very deliberately'.

Scendere. Add: *scendere a* (in travelling), 'to go to, put up at, a hotel'. Cf. the sentence from Fogazzaro, § 12 note.

Scorno. Note that *avere scorno di qualche cosa* means 'to be scorned for something'; 'to scorn' is *avere a scorno.*

Secolare. H. 'as E.', presumably in the sense of 'secular' as against 'religious' (Fr. *séculier*). But *secolare* has also the sense of 'age-old' (Fr. *séculaire*).

Secondare. Is not used for 'seconding a motion' (*appoggiare una proposta*).

Secondo, preposition ('according to'). Note the elliptic use: *È secondo,* 'It depends (on circumstances)'. Cf. French *C'est selon.*

Sereno. H. (1) 'serene'. Is used of the sky or season or day more freely than we should use 'serene', and without any suggestion that a human quality is being transferred to things.

Simpatico. Given by H. merely as derivative of *simpatia,* 'sympathy'. But *simpatico* does not mean 'sympathetic'; it is the commonest of conventional words of praise for persons and their behaviour, corresponding closely to colloquial English 'nice' ('likeable', 'attractive'). There is no single word in Italian for 'sympathetic'; among possibilities are *pronto a compatire, pieno di simpatia, indulgente* (*a una richiesta*).

Soggezione. Add the sense: 'embarrassment'.

Solenne. H. 'solemn'. Add the senses (a) 'eminent' (rather old-fashioned, but used in Carducci's prose); (b) 'terrific' (scolding, quarrel, price, blow); very common in familiar language. *E ripresa l' ascia in mano, tirò giù un solennissimo colpo sul pezzo di legno.* (Collodi.)

Sopportare. H. 'as E.' Rather 'to bear, stand, put up with'. 'He can't support his wife', *non può mantenere (sostentare) la moglie. Non può sopportare la moglie,* 'he can't abide her'.

Sorridere. Add the sense: 'please, attract'. *Quest' idea mi sorride.*

Spinace. H. 'spinach'. In botany, yes. In cookery, always plural, *gli spinaci.*

Squallido. H. 'as E.' On the contrary, it may be doubted if *squallido* ever means 'squalid'. Petrocchi defines it: *D' apparenza lugubre, trista*; and it corresponds to such English words as 'grim, dismal, dreary, lack-lustre, dour, grisly, ghastly'. A *stanza squallida* is a 'cheerless room', which may or may not be dirty (whereas 'a squalid hovel' is *un lurido abituro*). *Scogliere squallide*='gaunt reefs'; *sorriso squallido*='wan smile'.

Squattrinato='penniless'. Not in H.

Squisito. H. 'exquisite'. Italian and English correspond for 'exquisite' taste, courtesy, etc. But for food and wines *squisito* is nearer 'delicious' or 'delicate'; and on the other hand 'exquisite flowers', 'an exquisite house' are *fiori deliziosi, una casa deliziosa.*

Stupido. H. 'as E.' No, the Italian is very much stronger (roughly ='imbecile'); one may call oneself *stupido* on occasion, but applied to others the word is most insulting. 'Stupid'=*sciocco, insulso, stolido.* ('Stolid'=*inerte, spassionato,* etc.)

Vasto. H. 'as E.' No, the Italian is not so strong; 'wide, ample, extensive'.

Visitare. H. 'as E.' It is rarely used of a purely social visit[1] (which is *passare da, andare a trovare*); but it is the normal word for someone visiting the sick, a priest visiting his parishioners, a tourist visiting an art gallery. It also has the sense of EXAMINATION by a customs official or by a doctor. When the present Pope had a slight accident, the English papers reported that he had been 'visited' by his physician (a diplomatic as well as linguistic *topica*, for a commoner does not 'visit' a sovereign). The Italian papers of course had said that the Pope was *visitato,* i.e. examined or 'seen'.

[1] The noun *visita* is commoner in this sense.

Volere. Add the sense: 'should (be), is (to be)', with *essere* and an adjective or a passive. *Tale vuol essere la condotta...*, 'Such should be the behaviour...'; *Questo vuol essere fatto (inteso) così*, 'It is to be done (understood) thus'; *Amico e vino voglion esser vecchi*, 'Friends and wine had best be old'. And note that *volere*, especially in the past definite, may be stronger than 'wish' or 'want'. *Stavo per partire, ma egli mi volle ritenere*, 'he **would** keep me' or 'he insisted on keeping me'.

Volta. Add: *una buona volta*, 'once and for all'.

§ 95. Accentuation.

H. gives the accentuation *confraternità* ('a religious confraternity'); this should be *confratérnita* (plural *confraternite*). *Fraternita* too may set back its accent if it has the same sense; but in the ordinary abstract sense ('brotherliness'), H.'s *fraternità* is alone correct.

The difference between 'pariah' and 'peerage' should be marked by accent as well as gender. *Il pária* = 'pariah'; *la paría* = 'peerage'.

IX

PUNCTUATION

§ 96. There is now less difference than there once was between Italian and English punctuation (see the note and example in Hoare, s.v. *Punteggiatura*). But Italian usage is still worth noting on certain points.

(a) Commas are often omitted between words that form a parallel series.

> *Tutto cotesto viveva ardeva fremeva sotto il regno del sole nel cielo incandescente.* (Carducci.)

> *Contendendo per un quattrino con beccai mugnai e fornaciai.* (Carducci.)

> *Era deciso...di ripartire ritornare in città mettersi a fare un mestiere come tutti gli altri.* (Comisso.)

(b) The subject of a sentence is often marked off by commas even when there is no break in the sense.

> *La sora Flaminia, lo prevenne....* (Fucini.)

> *Un busto di marmo sopra una colonnetta di bardiglio, sarebbe costato duemila lire circa.* (Fucini.)

> *Le ragazze, studiavano anche il pianoforte.* (Pea.)

(c) A comma sometimes precedes a relative even when this is restrictive or partitive. In English there is an elementary distinction between (A) 'Painting which is irrational' and (B) 'Painting, which is irrational'; between (A) 'Women who are intelligent' and (B) 'Women, who are intelligent'. In Italian some quite good writers use a comma in the (A) sentences.

> *Non vi sono che i veri amici, che sappiano rendere di questi grandi favori.* (Collodi.)
> It's only real friends who will do such favours.

Rido di quei barbagianni, che credono a tutte le scioccherie.
   (Collodi.)
I'm laughing at the simpletons who listen to any nonsense.

Era una medicina, che accumulandosi nel sangue si trasformava
   in veleno. (Piovene.)
It was a medicine that turned to poison....

Fra poche ore sarebbero giunti in un paese, dove non c' erano
   nè libri, nè scuole, nè maestri. (Collodi.)
...a country where there were no books or schools or school-
   masters.

INDEX

References are by pages, indices denoting footnotes

INDEX